WORKING PAPERS FOR USE WITH

Fundamental Accounting Principles

VOLUME 2

TENTH CANADIAN EDITION
CHAPTERS 12–20

KERMIT D. LARSON
University of Texas at Austin, Emeritus

TILLY JENSEN
Northern Alberta Institute of Technology

RAY CARROLL
Dalhousie University

Prepared by
TILLY JENSEN
Northern Alberta Institute of Technology

McGraw-Hill
Ryerson

Toronto Montréal Boston Burr Ridge, IL Dubuque, IA Madison, WI New York San Francisco
St. Louis Bangkok Bogotá Caracas Kuala Lumpur Lisbon London Madrid
Mexico City Milan New Delhi Santiago Seoul Singapore Sydney Taipei

McGraw-Hill
Ryerson Limited

A Subsidiary of The McGraw-Hill Companies

Working Papers for use with
Fundamental Accounting Principles
Volume II—chapters 12-20
Tenth Canadian Edition

ISBN: 0-07-088989-9

1 2 3 4 5 6 7 8 9 10 MP 0 9 8 7 6 5 4 3 2

Printed and bound in Canada.

Vice President, Editorial Director: Pat Ferrier
Senior Sponsoring Editor: Nicole Lukach
Developmental Editor: Katherine Goodes
Supervising Editor: Alissa Messner
Senior Marketing Manager: Jeff MacLean
Production Coordinator: Madeleine Harrington
Printer: Maracle Press

Contents

Quick Study 12-11

_____
_____
_____
_____
_____

Quick Study 12-12

GENERAL JOURNAL   Page____

Date	Account Titles and Explanation	PR	Debit	Credit

GENERAL JOURNAL   Page____

Date	Account Titles and Explanation	PR	Debit	Credit
a.				
b.				
c.				

Quick Study 12-14

GENERAL JOURNAL   Page____

Date	Account Titles and Explanation	PR	Debit	Credit

Quick Study 12-15

GENERAL JOURNAL   Page____

Date	Account Titles and Explanation	PR	Debit	Credit
a.				
b.				

GENERAL JOURNAL   Page____

Date	Account Titles and Explanation	PR	Debit	Credit

Quick Study 12-17

GENERAL JOURNAL   Page____

Date	Account Titles and Explanation	PR	Debit	Credit

Exercise 12-1

Name _____

_____

_____

_____

_____

_____

_____

_____

Journal entry:

GENERAL JOURNAL   Page____

Date	Account Titles and Explanation	PR	Debit	Credit

Exercise 12-3

Cost of land:

_____

_____

_____

_____

_____

_____

Cost of building:

_____

_____

_____

_____

Journal entry:

GENERAL JOURNAL   Page____

Date	Account Titles and Explanation	PR	Debit	Credit

Year	Straight-line	Double-declining balance
2001		
2002		
2003		
2004		

Exercise 12-5

Year	Units-of-production
2001	
2002	
2003	
2004	

Exercise 12-6

a. _____

b. _____

c. _____

Year	Straight-Line Method		Double-Declining Balance Method	
	Amortization Expense	Book Value at December 31	Amortization Expense	Book Value at December 31
2001				
2002				
2003				
2004				

Exercise 12-8

Year	Units-of-Production Method	
	Amortization Expense	Book Value at December 31
2001		
2002		
2003		
2004		

a.

	Cost Information					Amortization		
Description	Date of Purchase	Amortization Method	Cost	Salvage	Life	Balance of Accum. Amort. Dec. 31, 2000	Amortization Expense for 2001	Balance of Accum. Amort. Dec. 31, 2001

b.

Creo Products
Partial Balance Sheet
December 31, 2000

Exercise 12-11

a.

	Year 1	Year 2	Year 3	Year 4	Year 5
Income before amortization					
Amortization expense					
Net income					

b.

	Year 1	Year 2	Year 3	Year 4	Year 5
Income before amortization					
Amortization expense					
Net income					

Year	Amortization	
	Straight-Line	**Double-Declining-Balance**
2001		
2002		
2003		
Totals		

Exercise 12-13

Year	Units-of-Production Amortization	
2001		
2002		
2003		
Total		

Year	Amortization		
	Straight-Line	**Double-Declining-Balance**	**Units-of-Production**
2001			
2002			
2003			
2004			

Exercise 12-15

Year	Amortization		
	Straight-Line	**Double-Declining-Balance**	**Units-of-Production**
2001			
2002			
2003			
2004			

Chapter 12   **Exercise 12-16**   *Name* _____

a. _____

_____

_____

b. _____

_____

_____

Exercise 12-17

a. _____

_____

_____

b. _____

_____

_____

Exercise 12-18

GENERAL JOURNAL   Page____

Date	Account Titles and Explanation	PR	Debit		Credit	

Calculations:

GENERAL JOURNAL   Page____

Date	Account Titles and Explanation	PR	Debit	Credit

Exercise 12-20

a. _____

_____

b. _____

GENERAL JOURNAL   Page____

Date	Account Titles and Explanation	PR	Debit	Credit

c. _____

d. _____

GENERAL JOURNAL   Page____

Date	Account Titles and Explanation	PR	Debit	Credit

GENERAL JOURNAL   Page____

Date	Account Titles and Explanation	PR	Debit	Credit
a.				
b.				
c.				

Exercise 12-22

Partial year's amortization:

GENERAL JOURNAL   Page____

Date	Account Titles and Explanation	PR	Debit	Credit

GENERAL JOURNAL   Page____

	Date	Account Titles and Explanation	PR	Debit			Credit		
a.									
b.									

Exercise 12-23

a. _____

b. _____

_____

c. _____

_____

Exercise 12-24

GENERAL JOURNAL   Page____

	Date	Account Titles and Explanation	PR	Debit			Credit		
a.									
b.									

Chapter 12   *Exercise 12-29   **Name** _____

GENERAL JOURNAL   Page____

Date	Account Titles and Explanation	PR	Debit	Credit

Problem 12-1A

Part 1

	Land	Building Two	Building Three	Land Improv. One	Land Improv. Two
Purchase price					
Demolition............ ...					
Landscaping					
New building					
New improvements .					
Totals					

Calculations:

Part 2

GENERAL JOURNAL   Page____

Date	Account Titles and Explanation	PR	Debit	Credit

Year	Amortization		
	Straight-Line	**Double-Declining-Balance**	**Units-of-Production**
2001			
2002			
2003			

Problem 12-3A

Year	Amortization		
	Straight-Line	**Double-Declining-Balance**	**Units-of-Production**
2001			
2002			
2003			

Name _____

1. **Double-declining-balance method**   <u>2001</u>   <u>2002</u>   <u>2003</u>
   Equipment .... _____ _____ _____
   Less: Accumulated amortization ..... _____ _____ _____
   Year-end book value......................... _____ _____ _____
   Amortization expense for the year.... _____ _____ _____

2. **Straight-line method**   <u>2001</u>   <u>2002</u>   <u>2003</u>
   Equipment .... _____ _____ _____
   Less: Accumulated amortization ..... _____ _____ _____
   Year-end book value......................... _____ _____ _____
   Amortization expense for the year.... _____ _____ _____

Calculations:

Problem 12-5A

GENERAL JOURNAL   Page____

Date	Account Titles and Explanation	PR	Debit	Credit

Part 1

	Appraised Value	Percent of Total	Apportioned Cost
Building			
Land................................			
Land improvements..........			
Vehicles			
Total................................			

GENERAL JOURNAL   Page____

Date	Account Titles and Explanation	PR	Debit	Credit

Part 2

_____
_____
_____
_____

Part 3

_____
_____
_____
_____

Name _____

Year	Amortization		
	Straight-Line	Double-Declining-Balance	Units-of-Production
2001			
2002			
2003			
2004			
2005			
Totals			

Calculations:

Cost Information						Amortization		
Description	Date of Purchase	Amortization Method	Cost	Salvage	Life	Balance of Accum. Amort. Dec. 31, 2000	Amortization Expense for 2001	Balance of Accum. Amort. Dec. 31, 2001

Calculations:

Name _____

GENERAL JOURNAL   Page____

Date	Account Titles and Explanation	PR	Debit	Credit

Problem 12-10A

GENERAL JOURNAL   Page____

Date	Account Titles and Explanation	PR	Debit	Credit

GENERAL JOURNAL

Page____

Date	Account Titles and Explanation	PR	Debit	Credit

Calculations:

GENERAL JOURNAL   Page____

Date	Account Titles and Explanation	PR	Debit		Credit	

Calculations:

Problem 12-13A

1.

GENERAL JOURNAL   Page____

Date	Account Titles and Explanation	PR	Debit		Credit	

1. (continued)

GENERAL JOURNAL   Page____

Date		Account Titles and Explanation	PR	Debit	Credit

2.

GENERAL JOURNAL   Page____

Date		Account Titles and Explanation	PR	Debit	Credit

3a.

GENERAL JOURNAL   Page____

Date		Account Titles and Explanation	PR	Debit	Credit

3b.

GENERAL JOURNAL   Page____

Date		Account Titles and Explanation	PR	Debit		Credit	

3c.

GENERAL JOURNAL   Page____

Date		Account Titles and Explanation	PR	Debit		Credit	

Calculations:

GENERAL JOURNAL   Page____

Date	Account Titles and Explanation	PR	Debit	Credit

Problem 12-15A

a. and c. Purchase and disposal of each machine:

GENERAL JOURNAL   Page____

Date	Account Titles and Explanation	PR	Debit	Credit

a. and c. (continued)

GENERAL JOURNAL   Page____

Date	Account Titles and Explanation	PR	Debit	Credit

b. Amortization expense on first December 31 of each machine's life:

GENERAL JOURNAL   Page____

Date	Account Titles and Explanation	PR	Debit	Credit

Calculations:

GENERAL JOURNAL   Page____

Date	Account Titles and Explanation	PR	Debit	Credit
a.				
b.				
c.				
d.				

Problem 12-17A

GENERAL JOURNAL   Page____

Date	Account Titles and Explanation	PR	Debit	Credit
a.				
b.				

1.

_____
_____
_____
_____
_____
_____

2.

GENERAL JOURNAL   Page____

Date	Account Titles and Explanation	PR	Debit	Credit

Problem 12-1B

Part 1

	Land	Building B	Building C	Land Improv. B	Land Improv. C
Purchase price					
Demolition............ ...					
Landscaping					
New building					
New improvements .					
Totals					

Calculations:

Part 2

GENERAL JOURNAL Page____

Date	Account Titles and Explanation	PR	Debit	Credit

Fundamental Accounting Principles, 10th Canadian Edition

Year	Amortization		
	Straight-Line	Double-Declining-Balance	Units-of-Production
2001			
2002			
2003			

Problem 12-3B

Year	Amortization		
	Straight-Line	Double-Declining-Balance	Units-of-Production
2001			
2002			
2003			

Name _____

a. **Double-declining-balance method**   2001   2002   2003
   Equipment .... _____ _____ _____
   Less: Accumulated amortization ..... _____ _____ _____
   Year-end book value .... _____ _____ _____
   Amortization expense for the year .... _____ _____ _____

b. **Straight-line method**   2001   2002   2003
   Equipment .... _____ _____ _____
   Less: Accumulated amortization ..... _____ _____ _____
   Year-end book value .... _____ _____ _____
   Amortization expense for the year .... _____ _____ _____

Calculations:

Problem 12-5B

GENERAL JOURNAL   Page____

Date	Account Titles and Explanation	PR	Debit	Credit

Name _____

	Appraised Value	Percent of Total	Apportioned Cost
Building..............................			
Land..................................			
Land improvements...........			
Vehicles............................	_____	_____	_____
Total.................................	_____	_____	_____

GENERAL JOURNAL   Page____

Date	Account Titles and Explanation	PR	Debit	Credit

Part 2

_____

_____

_____

_____

Part 3

_____

_____

_____

_____

Year	Amortization		
	Straight-Line	**Double-Declining-Balance**	**Units-of-Production**
2001			
2002			
2003			
2004			
2005			
2006			
Totals			

Calculations:

Cost Information						Amortization		
Description	Date of Purchase	Amortization Method	Cost	Salvage	Life	Balance of Accum. Amort. Dec. 31, 2000	Amortization Expense for 2001	Balance of Accum. Amort. Dec. 31, 2001

Calculations:

GENERAL JOURNAL   Page____

Date	Account Titles and Explanation	PR	Debit	Credit

Calculations:

Name _____

GENERAL JOURNAL

Page____

Date		Account Titles and Explanation	PR	Debit			Credit		

Calculations:

GENERAL JOURNAL   Page____

Date	Account Titles and Explanation	PR	Debit	Credit

Name _____

GENERAL JOURNAL   Page____

Date		Account Titles and Explanation	PR	Debit		Credit	

Calculations:

Problem 12-13B

1.

GENERAL JOURNAL   Page____

Date		Account Titles and Explanation	PR	Debit		Credit	

GENERAL JOURNAL   Page____

Date	Account Titles and Explanation	PR	Debit	Credit

2.

GENERAL JOURNAL   Page____

Date	Account Titles and Explanation	PR	Debit	Credit

3a.

GENERAL JOURNAL   Page____

Date	Account Titles and Explanation	PR	Debit	Credit

Name

_____

3b.

GENERAL JOURNAL   Page____

Date	Account Titles and Explanation	PR	Debit	Credit

3c.

GENERAL JOURNAL   Page____

Date	Account Titles and Explanation	PR	Debit	Credit

Calculations:

© 2002 McGraw-Hill Ryerson Limited.

GENERAL JOURNAL   Page____

Date	Account Titles and Explanation	PR	Debit	Credit

Problem 12-15B

a. and c. Purchase and disposal of each machine:

GENERAL JOURNAL   Page____

Date	Account Titles and Explanation	PR	Debit	Credit

a. and c. (continued)

GENERAL JOURNAL   Page____

Date	Account Titles and Explanation	PR	Debit	Credit

Calculations:

b. Amortization expense on first December 31 of each machine's life:

GENERAL JOURNAL   Page____

Date	Account Titles and Explanation	PR	Debit	Credit

Calculations:

GENERAL JOURNAL   Page____

Date		Account Titles and Explanation	PR	Debit	Credit
a.					
b.					
c.					
d.					

Problem 12-17B

GENERAL JOURNAL   Page____

Date		Account Titles and Explanation	PR	Debit	Credit
a.					
b.					

GENERAL JOURNAL   Page____

Date	Account Titles and Explanation	PR	Debit	Credit
c.				
d.				
e.				

Problem 12-18B

1.

_____

_____

_____

2.

GENERAL JOURNAL   Page____

Date	Account Titles and Explanation	PR	Debit	Credit

Current Liabilities:

_____
_____

Quick Study 13-2

a.

_____
_____
_____
_____
_____
_____
_____

b.

_____
_____
_____
_____
_____
_____

Quick Study 13-3

GENERAL JOURNAL   Page____

Date	Account Titles and Explanation	PR	Debit	Credit

GENERAL JOURNAL   Page____

Date	Account Titles and Explanation	PR	Debit	Credit

Quick Study 13-5

GENERAL JOURNAL   Page____

Date	Account Titles and Explanation	PR	Debit	Credit

Quick Study 13-6

GENERAL JOURNAL   Page____

Date	Account Titles and Explanation	PR	Debit	Credit

GENERAL JOURNAL   Page____

Date	Account Titles and Explanation	PR	Debit	Credit

Quick Study 13-8

GENERAL JOURNAL   Page____

Date	Account Titles and Explanation	PR	Debit	Credit

Quick Study 13-9

_____

_____

_____

_____

Quick Study 13-10

GENERAL JOURNAL   Page____

Date	Account Titles and Explanation	PR	Debit	Credit

Name _____

GENERAL JOURNAL   Page____

Date		Account Titles and Explanation	PR	Debit				Credit			

Quick Study 13-12

GENERAL JOURNAL   Page____

Date		Account Titles and Explanation	PR	Debit				Credit			

Quick Study 13-13

1. _____

2. _____

3. _____

Quick Study 13-14

GENERAL JOURNAL   Page____

Date		Account Titles and Explanation	PR	Debit				Credit			

GENERAL JOURNAL   Page____

Date	Account Titles and Explanation	PR	Debit	Credit

*Quick Study 13-16

GENERAL JOURNAL   Page____

Date	Account Titles and Explanation	PR	Debit	Credit

Exercise 13-1

a. _____   e. _____
b. _____   f. _____
c. _____   g. _____
d. _____   h. _____

Kotler Company
Partial Balance Sheet
December 31, 2001

Exercise 3-3

1a.

GENERAL JOURNAL Page_____

Date	Account Titles and Explanation	PR	Debit	Credit

1b.

GENERAL JOURNAL Page_____

Date	Account Titles and Explanation	PR	Debit	Credit

2.

Estrada Company
Partial Balance Sheet
December 31, 2001

Exercise 13-5

GENERAL JOURNAL   Page____

Date	Account Titles and Explanation	PR	Debit	Credit

a.   GENERAL JOURNAL   Page____

Date	Account Titles and Explanation	PR	Debit	Credit

b.   GENERAL JOURNAL   Page____

Date	Account Titles and Explanation	PR	Debit	Credit

c.   GENERAL JOURNAL   Page____

Date	Account Titles and Explanation	PR	Debit	Credit

Exercise 13-7

a.   GENERAL JOURNAL   Page____

Date	Account Titles and Explanation	PR	Debit	Credit

b.   **GENERAL JOURNAL**   Page____

Date	Account Titles and Explanation	PR	Debit	Credit

c.   **GENERAL JOURNAL**   Page____

Date	Account Titles and Explanation	PR	Debit	Credit

Exercise 13-8

a.

_____

_____

_____

_____

_____

_____

b.

_____

_____

_____

c.

GENERAL JOURNAL   Page____

Date	Account Titles and Explanation	PR	Debit	Credit

Exercise 13-9

a.

_____

_____

_____

_____

_____

_____

_____

_____

b.

_____

_____

c.

_____

_____

d.

GENERAL JOURNAL   Page____

Date	Account Titles and Explanation	PR	Debit	Credit

_____

GENERAL JOURNAL   Page____

Date	Account Titles and Explanation	PR	Debit	Credit

Exercise 13-10

a.

	Jan. – Mar.	Apr. – June	July – Sept.	Oct. – Dec.
Income before tax				
Estimated income tax expense......				
Net income				

b.

GENERAL JOURNAL   Page____

Date	Account Titles and Explanation	PR	Debit	Credit

c.

GENERAL JOURNAL   Page____

Date	Account Titles and Explanation	PR	Debit	Credit

d.

_____
_____
_____

a.

GENERAL JOURNAL   Page____

Date		Account Titles and Explanation	PR	Debit	Credit

b.

GENERAL JOURNAL   Page____

Date		Account Titles and Explanation	PR	Debit	Credit

c.

_____

_____

d.

_____

_____

Exercise 13-12

a.

_____

_____

b.

_____

_____

c.

_____

_____

d.

_____

_____

_____

_____

_____

_____

e. Journal entries:

GENERAL JOURNAL   Page____

Date	Account Titles and Explanation	PR	Debit	Credit

Exercise 13-13

1.

_____

_____

_____

_____

2.

GENERAL JOURNAL   Page____

Date	Account Titles and Explanation	PR	Debit	Credit

Name _____

GENERAL JOURNAL   Page____

Date	Account Titles and Explanation	PR	Debit	Credit

Exercise 13-14

1.

GENERAL JOURNAL   Page____

Date	Account Titles and Explanation	PR	Debit	Credit

2.

_____

_____

_____

3.

GENERAL JOURNAL   Page____

Date	Account Titles and Explanation	PR	Debit	Credit

4.   GENERAL JOURNAL   Page____

Date	Account Titles and Explanation	PR	Debit	Credit

*Exercise 13-15

a.

_____

_____

_____

_____

_____

_____

_____

_____

_____

_____

b.

_____

_____

c.

                          GENERAL JOURNAL   Page____

Date	Account Titles and Explanation	PR	Debit	Credit

a.

_____
_____
_____
_____
_____
_____
_____
_____
_____
_____

b.

_____
_____

c.

_____
_____

d.

GENERAL JOURNAL   Page____

Date	Account Titles and Explanation	PR	Debit	Credit

Name _____

	December 31,		
2002	2003	2004	2005

_____
_____
_____
_____
_____
_____
_____
_____
_____

Problem 13-2A

1.

Maturity dates:	Franken, Inc.	Bank of the North	Maritime Bank
Date of the note......................			
Term of the note...................			
Maturity date			

2.

GENERAL JOURNAL   Page____

Date	Account Titles and Explanation	PR	Debit	Credit

Name _____

GENERAL JOURNAL   Page____

Date	Account Titles and Explanation	PR	Debit	Credit

Problem 13-3A

1. Warranty expense for November and December 2002:

_____

_____

_____

_____

_____

2. Warranty expense for January 2003:

_____

_____

_____

_____

_____

3. Balance of the estimated liability as of December 31, 2002:

_____

_____

_____

_____

_____

4. Balance of the estimated liability as of January 31, 2003:

_____

_____

_____

_____

_____

_____

5.

GENERAL JOURNAL   Page____

Date	Account Titles and Explanation	PR	Debit	Credit

GENERAL JOURNAL   Page____

Date	Account Titles and Explanation	PR	Debit	Credit

Problem 13-4A

1.

GENERAL JOURNAL   Page____

Date	Account Titles and Explanation	PR	Debit	Credit

Name

GENERAL JOURNAL   Page____

Date		Account Titles and Explanation	PR	Debit	Credit

2.

GENERAL JOURNAL   Page____

Date	Account Titles and Explanation	PR	Debit	Credit

Chapter 13   Problem 13-1B

	December 31,		
2002	2003	2004	2005

Name _____

GENERAL JOURNAL

Page____

Date	Account Titles and Explanation	PR	Debit	Credit

GENERAL JOURNAL   Page____

Date	Account Titles and Explanation	PR	Debit	Credit

Problem 13-3B

1. **Warranty expense for November and December 2002:**

_____
_____
_____
_____
_____

2. **Warranty expense for January 2003:**

_____
_____
_____
_____
_____

3. **Balance of the estimated liability as of December 31, 2002:**

_____
_____
_____
_____
_____

4. Balance of the estimated liability as of January 31, 2003:

_____

_____

_____

_____

_____

_____

5.

GENERAL JOURNAL   Page____

Date	Account Titles and Explanation	PR	Debit	Credit

Name

GENERAL JOURNAL   Page____

Date	Account Titles and Explanation	PR	Debit	Credit

Problem 13-4B

To: Sue Peebles, General Manager

From: Sam Aryee, Manager, Accounting and Finance

Subject: Reporting contingencies and estimates in the financial statements

_____

_____

_____

_____

_____

_____

Comprehensive Problem
Part 1

(a) Correct Ending Balance of Cash and the Amount of the Omitted Cheque:

(b) Allowance for Doubtful Accounts:

(c) Amortization Expense on the Truck:

(d) Amortization Expense on the Equipment:

(e) Correct Revenue and Unearned Revenue Balances: _____

_____

_____

_____

_____

_____

_____

_____

_____

_____

_____

_____

_____

_____

_____

(f) Warranty Expense and Warranty Liability: _____

_____

_____

_____

_____

_____

_____

_____

(g) Discount on Note Payable and Interest Expense: _____

_____

_____

_____

_____

_____

_____

(h) Cost of Goods Sold: _____

_____

_____

_____

_____

FAST EXTERMINATORS
Six-Column Table
December 31, 2002

Account Titles	Unadjusted Trial Balance Dr.	Unadjusted Trial Balance Cr.	Adjustments Dr.	Adjustments Cr.	Adjusted Trial Balance Dr.	Adjusted Trial Balance Cr.
Cash						
Accounts receivable						
Allowance for doubtful accounts						
Merchandise inventory						
Trucks						
Accumulated amortization, trucks						
Equipment						
Accum. amortization, equipment						
Accounts payable						
Estimated warranty liability						
Unearned services revenue						
Long-term notes payable						
Ken Jones, capital						
Ken Jones, withdrawals						
Extermination services revenue						
Interest earned						
Sales						
Cost of goods sold						
Amortization expense, trucks						
Amortization expense, equipment						
Wages expense						
Interest expense						
Rent expense						
Bad debts expense						
Miscellaneous expense						
Repairs expense						
Utilities expense						
Warranty expense						
Totals						

GENERAL JOURNAL

Page_____

Date	Account Titles and Explanation	PR	Debit	Credit

FAST EXTERMINATORS
Income Statement
For Year Ended December 31, 2002

FAST EXTERMINATORS
Statement of Owner's Equity
For Year Ended December 31, 2002

FAST EXTERMINATORS
Balance Sheet
December 31, 2002

Name _____

_____
_____
_____
_____
_____
_____
_____
_____
_____
_____

Quick Study 14-2

_____
_____
_____
_____
_____

Quick Study 14-3

GENERAL JOURNAL   Page____

Date	Account Titles and Explanation	PR	Debit	Credit

Quick Study 14-4

	Share to Ace	Share to Bud	Total

_____
_____
_____
_____
_____
_____
_____
_____
_____
_____

	Share to Blythe	Share to Beery	Total

Quick Study 14-6

GENERAL JOURNAL   Page____

Date	Account Titles and Explanation	PR	Debit	Credit

Calculations:

	Share to Montgomery	Share to Calmar	Total

Name _____

GENERAL JOURNAL   Page____

Date	Account Titles and Explanation	PR	Debit	Credit

Calculations:

	Share to Montgomery	Share to Calmar	Total

_____

_____

_____

_____

_____

_____

_____

_____

_____

_____

_____

_____

_____

Quick Study 14-8

GENERAL JOURNAL   Page____

Date	Account Titles and Explanation	PR	Debit	Credit

Name _____

Calculations:

	Share to Montgomery	Share to Calmar	Total

Quick Study 14-9

GENERAL JOURNAL   Page____

Date	Account Titles and Explanation	PR	Debit	Credit

Quick Study 14-10

GENERAL JOURNAL   Page____

Date	Account Titles and Explanation	PR	Debit	Credit

Name _____

GENERAL JOURNAL   Page____

Date	Account Titles and Explanation	PR	Debit	Credit

Quick Study 14-12

GENERAL JOURNAL   Page____

Date	Account Titles and Explanation	PR	Debit	Credit

Quick Study 14-13

GENERAL JOURNAL   Page____

Date	Account Titles and Explanation	PR	Debit	Credit

Quick Study 14-14

GENERAL JOURNAL   Page____

Date	Account Titles and Explanation	PR	Debit	Credit

Name _____

GENERAL JOURNAL   Page____

Date	Account Titles and Explanation	PR	Debit	Credit

Quick Study 14-16

_____

_____

_____

_____

_____

_____

_____

Quick Study 14-17

GENERAL JOURNAL   Page____

Date	Account Titles and Explanation	PR	Debit	Credit

Calculations:

	Cash	Other Assets	Sam, Capital	Andrews, Capital	Mary, Capital

Name _____

GENERAL JOURNAL

Page____

Date	Account Titles and Explanation	PR	Debit	Credit

Calculations:

	Cash	Other Assets	Sam, Capital	Andrews, Capital	Mary, Capital

Exercise 14-1

1.

2.

3.

a.

GENERAL JOURNAL

Page____

Date	Account Titles and Explanation	PR	Debit	Credit

Name _____

Calculations:

	Share to Young	Share to Olde	Total

b.
Capital account balances:

	Young	Olde

Exercise 14-3

a.

	Share to Newton	Share to Scampi	Total

b.

	Share to Newton	Share to Scampi	Total

c.

	Share to Newton	Share to Scampi	Total

Exercise 14-4

a.

	Share to Newton	Share to Scampi	Total

b.

	Share to Newton	Share to Scampi	Total

Name _____

a.

GENERAL JOURNAL

Page____

Date		Account Titles and Explanation	PR	Debit			Credit		

Calculations:

	Share to Sauer	Share to Curtley	Total

b.

Capital account balances:

	Sauer	Curtley

Name _____

	Share to Alex	Share to Warren	Total

Calculations:

Exercise 14-7

a.   GENERAL JOURNAL   Page____

Date	Account Titles and Explanation	PR	Debit	Credit

b.   GENERAL JOURNAL   Page____

Date	Account Titles and Explanation	PR	Debit	Credit

c.   GENERAL JOURNAL   Page____

Date		Account Titles and Explanation	PR	Debit				Credit			

Calculations:

Exercise 14-8

                              GENERAL JOURNAL   Page____

Date		Account Titles and Explanation	PR	Debit				Credit			

Exercise 14-9

a.   GENERAL JOURNAL   Page____

Date		Account Titles and Explanation	PR	Debit				Credit			

b.   GENERAL JOURNAL   Page____

Date	Account Titles and Explanation	PR	Debit	Credit

c.   GENERAL JOURNAL   Page____

Date	Account Titles and Explanation	PR	Debit	Credit

Exercise 14-10

GENERAL JOURNAL   Page____

Date	Account Titles and Explanation	PR	Debit	Credit

Calculations:

	Cash	Equip.	Accum. Amort. Equip.	A/P	Notes Payable	Bill Weston, Capital	Marnie Wolf, Capital	Jacob Bean, Capital

Name _____

GENERAL JOURNAL   Page____

Date	Account Titles and Explanation	PR	Debit	Credit

Calculations:

	Cash	Bldg.	Accum. Amort. Bldg.	Land	A/P	Martha Wheaton, Capital	Bess Jones, Capital	Sam Dun, Capital

Exercise 14-12

GENERAL JOURNAL   Page____

Date	Account Titles and Explanation	PR	Debit	Credit

Calculations:

	Cash	Bldg.	Accum. Amort. Bldg.	Land	A/P	Martha Wheaton, Capital	Bess Jones, Capital	Sam Dun, Capital

Name _____

1.

	Whiz	Bam	Boom	Total

2.

GENERAL JOURNAL   Page____

Date	Account Titles and Explanation	PR	Debit	Credit

3.

GENERAL JOURNAL   Page____

Date	Account Titles and Explanation	PR	Debit	Credit

Name _____

a.

GENERAL JOURNAL   Page____

Date	Account Titles and Explanation	PR	Debit	Credit

b.

GENERAL JOURNAL   Page____

Date	Account Titles and Explanation	PR	Debit	Credit

c.

GENERAL JOURNAL   Page____

Date	Account Titles and Explanation	PR	Debit	Credit

Name

Calculations:

	Share to Carroll	Share to Lee	Share to Power	Total

Problem 14-2A

Income (Loss) Sharing Plan: Year 1

a.

	Share to Meade	Share to Munez	Total

b.

	Share to Meade	Share to Munez	Total

c.

	Share to Meade	Share to Munez	Total

Name _____

d.

	Share to Meade	Share to Munez	Total

Income (Loss) Sharing Plan: Year 2

a.

	Share to Meade	Share to Munez	Total

b.

	Share to Meade	Share to Munez	Total

c.

	Share to Meade	Share to Munez	Total

d.

	Share to Meade	Share to Munez	Total

Name _____

Income (Loss) Sharing Plan: Year 3

a.

	Share to Meade	Share to Munez	Total

b.

	Share to Meade	Share to Munez	Total

c.

	Share to Meade	Share to Munez	Total

d.

	Share to Meade	Share to Munez	Total

Problem 14-3A

Part 1

a.

	Share to Iris	Share to Dolan	Share to Carrow	Total

b.

	Share to Iris	Share to Dolan	Share to Carrow	Total

Fundamental Accounting Principles, 10th Canadian Edition

Name _____

c.

	Share to Iris	Share to Dolan	Share to Carrow	Total

Part 2

IDC PARTNERSHIP
Statement of Partners' Equity
For Year Ended December 31, 2002

	Iris	Dolan	Carrow	Total

Part 3

GENERAL JOURNAL   Page____

Date	Account Titles and Explanation	PR	Debit	Credit

Name _____

GENERAL JOURNAL   Page____

Date		Account Titles and Explanation	PR	Debit				Credit			

Problem 14-4A

a.

GENERAL JOURNAL   Page____

Date		Account Titles and Explanation	PR	Debit				Credit			

b.

GENERAL JOURNAL   Page____

Date		Account Titles and Explanation	PR	Debit				Credit			

Name _____

c.   GENERAL JOURNAL   Page____

Date	Account Titles and Explanation	PR	Debit	Credit

Problem 14-5A

a.   GENERAL JOURNAL   Page____

Date	Account Titles and Explanation	PR	Debit	Credit

b.   GENERAL JOURNAL   Page____

Date	Account Titles and Explanation	PR	Debit	Credit

c.   GENERAL JOURNAL   Page____

Date	Account Titles and Explanation	PR	Debit	Credit

d.   GENERAL JOURNAL   Page____

Date	Account Titles and Explanation	PR	Debit	Credit

e.   GENERAL JOURNAL   Page____

Date	Account Titles and Explanation	PR	Debit	Credit

Problem 14-6A

a.

	Cash	Other Assets	Accounts Payable	David Pyle, Capital	Annie White, Capital	Mike Zin, Capital

Calculations:

Name

b.

	Cash	Other Assets	Accounts Payable	David Pyle, Capital	Annie White, Capital	Mike Zin, Capital

Calculations:

c.

	Cash	Other Assets	Accounts Payable	David Pyle, Capital	Annie White, Capital	Mike Zin, Capital

Calculations:

Name

d.

	Cash	Other Assets	Accounts Payable	David Pyle, Capital	Annie White, Capital	Mike Zin, Capital

Calculations:

Name _____

a.

GENERAL JOURNAL   Page____

Date	Account Titles and Explanation	PR	Debit	Credit

b.

GENERAL JOURNAL   Page____

Date	Account Titles and Explanation	PR	Debit	Credit

c.

GENERAL JOURNAL   Page____

Date	Account Titles and Explanation	PR	Debit	Credit

Calculations:

	Share to Jones	Share to Rodgers	Share to Jackson	Total

Problem 14-2B

Income (Loss) Sharing Plan: Year 1

a.

	Share to Monroe	Share to Young	Total

b.

	Share to Monroe	Share to Young	Total

c.

	Share to Monroe	Share to Young	Total

Name _____

d.

	Share to Monroe	Share to Young	Total

Income (Loss) Sharing Plan: Year 2

a.

	Share to Monroe	Share to Young	Total

b.

	Share to Monroe	Share to Young	Total

c.

	Share to Monroe	Share to Young	Total

d.

	Share to Monroe	Share to Young	Total

Name

Income (Loss) Sharing Plan: Year 3

a.

	Share to Monroe	Share to Young	Total

b.

	Share to Monroe	Share to Young	Total

c.

	Share to Monroe	Share to Young	Total

d.

	Share to Monroe	Share to Young	Total

Problem 14-3B

Part 1

a.

	Share to Vacon	Share to Masters	Share to Ramos	Total

b.

	Share to Vacon	Share to Masters	Share to Ramos	Total

Name _____

c.

	Share to Vacon	Share to Masters	Share to Ramos	Total

Part 2

IDC PARTNERSHIP
Statement of Partners' Equity
For Year Ended December 31, 2002

	Vacon	Masters	Ramos	Total

Part 3

GENERAL JOURNAL   Page____

Date	Account Titles and Explanation	PR	Debit	Credit

© 2002 McGraw-Hill Ryerson Limited.

Name _____

GENERAL JOURNAL   Page____

Date		Account Titles and Explanation	PR	Debit		Credit	

Problem 14-4B

a.   GENERAL JOURNAL   Page____

Date		Account Titles and Explanation	PR	Debit		Credit	

b.   GENERAL JOURNAL   Page____

Date		Account Titles and Explanation	PR	Debit		Credit	

c.   GENERAL JOURNAL   Page____

Date	Account Titles and Explanation	PR	Debit	Credit

Problem 14-5B

a.   GENERAL JOURNAL   Page____

Date	Account Titles and Explanation	PR	Debit	Credit

b.   GENERAL JOURNAL   Page____

Date	Account Titles and Explanation	PR	Debit	Credit

c.   GENERAL JOURNAL   Page____

Date	Account Titles and Explanation	PR	Debit	Credit

Name

d.   **GENERAL JOURNAL**   Page____

Date	Account Titles and Explanation	PR	Debit	Credit

e.   **GENERAL JOURNAL**   Page____

Date	Account Titles and Explanation	PR	Debit	Credit

Problem 14-6B

a.

	Cash	Equip. (net)	Accounts Payable	Ernie Poppy, Capital	Lynn Sweetbean, Capital	Ned Olive, Capital

Calculations:

b.

	Cash	Equip. (net)	Accounts Payable	Ernie Poppy, Capital	Lynn Sweetbean, Capital	Ned Olive, Capital

Calculations:

c.

	Cash	Equip. (net)	Accounts Payable	Ernie Poppy, Capital	Lynn Sweetbean, Capital	Ned Olive, Capital

Calculations:

Name

_____

d.

	Cash	Equip. (net)	Accounts Payable	Ernie Poppy, Capital	Lynn Sweetbean, Capital	Ned Olive, Capital

Calculations:

_____

_____

Quick Study 15-2

	GENERAL JOURNAL			Page____

Date	Account Titles and Explanation	PR	Debit	Credit

Quick Study 15-3

Ludwig Ltd.
Income Statement
For Year Ended October 31, 2001

Quick Study 15-4

_____	Cash	_____	Preferred shares
_____	Common shares	_____	Retained earnings
_____	Dividends payable	_____	Preferred dividend payable
_____	Deficit	_____	Preferred shares, $5 noncumulative

FORM OF BUSINESS ORGANIZATION

<u>Sole Proprietorship</u>	<u>Corporation</u>

Cash.....................................
    Ian Smith, Capital ....

Cash.....................................
    Revenues ....

Expenses..................................
    Cash ....

Ian Smith, Withdrawals................
    Cash ....

Revenues....................................
    Income Summary.................

Income Summary.......................
    Expenses..............................

Income Summary.......................
    Ian Smith, Capital ....

Ian Smith, Capital.......................
    Ian Smith, Withdrawals ....

Cash...................................
    Common Shares............

Cash...................................
    Revenues....................

Expenses............................
    Cash...........................

Cash Dividends Declared........
    Cash...........................

Revenues............................
    Income Summary............

Income Summary..................
    Expenses.....................

Income Summary..................
    Retained Earnings...........

Retained Earnings..................
    Cash Dividends Declared..

Vision Consulting
Partial Balance Sheet
December 31, 2001

Vision Consulting Inc.
Partial Balance Sheet
December 31, 2001

Owner's Equity
  Ian Smith, capital

  Total owner's equity

Shareholders' Equity
  Common shares
  Retained earnings
  Total shareholders' equity

Quick Study 15-6

_____   *OR*   _____ **Retained Earnings**
_____

Chapter 15   Quick Study 15-7

Name _____

a. _____

b. _____

c. _____

Quick Study 15-8

GENERAL JOURNAL   Page____

Date		Account Titles and Explanation	PR	Debit			Credit		

Quick Study 15-9

a. _____

b. _____

c. _____

Quick Study 15-10

a.

GENERAL JOURNAL   Page____

Date		Account Titles and Explanation	PR	Debit			Credit		

b. _____

_____

Quick Study 15-11

GENERAL JOURNAL   Page____

Date		Account Titles and Explanation	PR	Debit			Credit		

GENERAL JOURNAL   Page____

Date		Account Titles and Explanation	PR	Debit	Credit

Quick Study 15-12

_____

_____

_____

_____

_____

Quick Study 15-13

_____

_____

_____

_____

_____

Quick Study 15-14

a. _____

_____

_____

_____

_____

b. _____

_____

c. _____

_____

d. _____

_____

e. _____

a.   GENERAL JOURNAL   Page____

Date	Account Titles and Explanation	PR	Debit	Credit

b.

Peter Puck Inc.
Statement of Retained Earnings
For Year Ended May 31, 2001

Name _____

a.

GENERAL JOURNAL

Page____

Date	Account Titles and Explanation	PR	Debit	Credit

b.

Morris Inc.
Statement of Retained Earnings
For Year Ended November 30, 2001

Name _____

a.   GENERAL JOURNAL   Page____

Date	Account Titles and Explanation	PR	Debit	Credit

b.

Velor Ltd.
Statement of Retained Earnings
For Year Ended August 31, 2001

		Debit	Credit

*Quick Study 15-18

a.   GENERAL JOURNAL   Page____

Date	Account Titles and Explanation	PR	Debit	Credit

b.   GENERAL JOURNAL   Page____

Date	Account Titles and Explanation	PR	Debit	Credit

_____
_____
_____
_____
_____
_____
_____
_____

Exercise 15-1

		Corporations	General Partnerships
1.	Life		
2.	Owners' liability		
3.	Legal status		
4.	Tax status of income		
5.	Owners' authority		
6.	Ease of formation		
7.	Transferability of ownership		
8.	Ability to raise large amounts of capital		

Exercise 15-2

a.   **GENERAL JOURNAL**   Page____

Date	Account Titles and Explanation	PR	Debit	Credit

Name _____

a.   GENERAL JOURNAL   Page____

Date	Account Titles and Explanation	PR	Debit	Credit

b.   GENERAL JOURNAL   Page____

Date	Account Titles and Explanation	PR	Debit	Credit

Name _____

a.

GENERAL JOURNAL

Page____

Date	Account Titles and Explanation	PR	Debit	Credit

b.

Lindsay Ltd.
Shareholder's Equity
January 31, 2001

c. _____

Name _____

a.

GENERAL JOURNAL

Page____

Date	Account Titles and Explanation	PR	Debit	Credit

b.

ABC Inc.
Shareholder's Equity
December 31, 2002

c.

_____

Name _____

GENERAL JOURNAL   Page____

	Date	Account Titles and Explanation	PR	Debit	Credit
a.					
b.					
c.					

Exercise 15-6

GENERAL JOURNAL   Page____

	Date	Account Titles and Explanation	PR	Debit	Credit
a.					
b.					
c.					

Exercise 15-7

GENERAL JOURNAL   Page____

Date	Account Titles and Explanation	PR	Debit	Credit

Name _____

GENERAL JOURNAL

Page____

Date	Account Titles and Explanation	PR	Debit	Credit

Exercise 15-9

1. _____

_____

_____

_____

_____

_____

_____

2.

_____   **OR** _____ **Retained Earnings** _____

_____

_____

_____

_____

_____

_____

_____

3.

MARITIME INC.
Statement of Retained Earnings
For Year Ended December 31, 2002

Exercise 15-10

A.

B.

C.

D.

E.

Exercise 15-11

1.

2.

3.

4.

5.

6.

7.

8.

Name _____

	Preferred	Common

2001: _____

_____

_____

_____

_____

2002: _____

_____

_____

_____

_____

2003: _____

_____

_____

_____

_____

2004: _____

_____

_____

_____

_____

Total for four years: _____

Name _____

	Preferred	Common

2001: _____

_____

_____

_____

2002: _____

_____

_____

_____

2003: _____

_____

_____

_____

2004: _____

_____

_____

_____

Total for four years: _____

Exercise 15-14

1.	4.
2.	5.
3.	6.

Exercise 15-15

a. _____

b. _____

_____

Name _____

1.

GENERAL JOURNAL   Page____

Date	Account Titles and Explanation	PR	Debit	Credit

2.

DWF
Shareholder's Equity
December 31, 2003

3. _____

4. _____

Name _____

a.

GENERAL JOURNAL

Page____

Date	Account Titles and Explanation	PR	Debit	Credit

Name

b.

ABC Inc.
Balance Sheet
October 31, 2001

GENERAL JOURNAL   Page __,___

Date	Account Titles and Explanation	PR	Debit	Credit
a.				
b.				
c.				
d.				
e.				

Fallingwood Tree Services Inc.
Shareholders' Equity
December 31, 2001

Name _____

a.

_____
_____
_____
_____
_____
_____
_____
_____
_____

b.

_____
_____
_____
_____
_____
_____
_____
_____
_____

Name _____

Southgate Inc.
Balance Sheet
March 31, 2001

_____
_____
_____
_____
_____
_____
_____
_____
_____
_____
_____
_____

Problem 15-3A

_____
_____
_____
_____
_____
_____
_____
_____
_____
_____
_____

Problem 15-4A

1. _____

2. _____

3. _____

4. _____

5. _____

6a. _____

6b. _____

7a. _____

_____

7b. _____

_____

8. _____

_____

9. _____

_____

Problem 15-5A

1.

Year	Preferred Dividends	Common Dividends	Total Dividends
1999			
2000			
2001			
Totals			

2. _____

_____

_____

_____

Problem 15-6A

1. Journal entries:

GENERAL JOURNAL   Page____

Date	Account Titles and Explanation	PR	Debit	Credit

Name _____

Part 1

GENERAL JOURNAL   Page____

Date	Account Titles and Explanation	PR	Debit	Credit

Part 2

TREVOR CORPORATION
Statement of Retained Earnings
For Year Ended December 31, 2002

Part 3

TREVOR CORPORATION
Shareholders' Equity
December 31, 2002

Problem 15-7A

Part 1

GENERAL JOURNAL   Page____

Date	Account Titles and Explanation	PR	Debit	Credit

Name

GENERAL JOURNAL   Page____

Date	Account Titles and Explanation	PR	Debit	Credit

Part 2

DOUCETTE COMPANY
Shareholders' Equity
January 31, 2003

Problem 15-8A

Part 1

GENERAL JOURNAL   Page____

Date	Account Titles and Explanation	PR	Debit	Credit

GENERAL JOURNAL   Page____

Date	Account Titles and Explanation	PR	Debit	Credit

Part 2

OPPONG CORPORATION
Statement of Retained Earnings
For Year Ended December 31, 2002

Part 3

OPPONG CORPORATION
Shareholders' Equity
December 31, 2002

*Problem 15-9A

1.

2.

3.

Name _____

4. _____

5. _____

6. _____

Name _____

7. _____

_____

_____

_____

_____

_____

_____

_____

_____

*Problem 15-10A

Part 1:

a.

Book value per common share:	Book value per preferred share:

b.

Book value per common share:	Book value per preferred share:

Part 2:

c.

Book value per common share:	Book value per preferred share:

d.

Book value per common share:	Book value per preferred share:

Part 3:

Book value per common share:	Book value per preferred share:

JenStar Inc.
Balance Sheet
October 31, 2001

_____
_____
_____
_____
_____
_____
_____
_____
_____
_____
_____
_____
_____
_____

Problem 15-3B

_____
_____
_____
_____
_____
_____
_____
_____
_____
_____
_____
_____
_____
_____

Problem 15-4B

1. _____
2. _____
3. _____
4. _____
5. _____
6. _____
7. _____

Name _____

a.

Year	Preferred Dividends	Common Dividends	Total Dividends
1999			
2000			
2001			
2002			

b.

Year	Preferred Dividends	Common Dividends	Total Dividends
1999			
2000			
2001			
2002			

Problem 15-6B

1. Journal entries:

GENERAL JOURNAL   Page____

Date	Account Titles and Explanation	PR	Debit	Credit

Name
_____

Part 1

GENERAL JOURNAL

Page____

Date	Account Titles and Explanation	PR	Debit	Credit

Part 2

CALDWELL CORP.
Statement of Retained Earnings
For Year Ended December 31, 2002

Name

Part 3

CALDWELL CORP.
Shareholders' Equity
December 31, 2002

Problem 15-7B

Part 1

GENERAL JOURNAL   Page____

Date	Account Titles and Explanation	PR	Debit	Credit

Name

GENERAL JOURNAL

Page____

Date	Account Titles and Explanation	PR	Debit	Credit

Part 2

SOLAR ENERGY COMPANY INC.
Statement of Retained Earnings
For Year Ended December 31, 2002

Part 3

SOLAR ENERGY COMPANY INC.
Shareholders' Equity
December 31, 2002

Problem 15-8B

Part 1

GENERAL JOURNAL   Page____

Date	Account Titles and Explanation	PR	Debit	Credit

Name

GENERAL JOURNAL

Page____

Date	Account Titles and Explanation	PR	Debit	Credit

Part 2

FRANCOIS CORP.
Statement of Retained Earnings
For Year Ended December 31, 2001

Part 3

FRANCOIS CORP.
Shareholders' Equity
December 31, 2001

Problem 15-9B

a.

b.

c.

Name _____

Part 1:

a.

Book value per common share:	Book value per preferred share:

b.

Book value per common share:	Book value per preferred share:

Part 2:

c.

Book value per common share:	Book value per preferred share:

d.

Book value per common share:	Book value per preferred share:

Part 3:

Book value per common share:	Book value per preferred share:

Name _____

Time Period	Outstanding Shares	Fraction of Year Outstanding	Weighted Average*

Round to the nearest whole share

Quick Study 16-9

Time Period	Outstanding Shares	Effect of Share Dividend	Fraction of Year Outstanding	Weighted Average*

Round to the nearest whole share

Quick Study 16-10

Time Period	Outstanding Shares	Effect of Share Dividend	Fraction of Year Outstanding	Weighted Average*

Round to the nearest whole share

Quick Study 16-11

a. _____
_____
_____
_____
_____
_____

b. _____
_____
_____
_____
_____
_____

Name _____

GENERAL JOURNAL   Page____

Date	Account Titles and Explanation	PR	Debit	Credit

*Quick Study 16-13

GENERAL JOURNAL   Page____

Date	Account Titles and Explanation	PR	Debit	Credit

*Quick Study 16-14

GENERAL JOURNAL   Page____

Date	Account Titles and Explanation	PR	Debit	Credit

Name _____

Wesson Company Ltd.
Income Statement
For Year Ended December 31, 2001

Exercise 16-2

a. _____

_____

_____

_____

b. _____

_____

_____

c. _____

_____

_____

Name _____

1. _____
2. _____
3. _____
4. _____
5. _____
6. _____
7. _____
8. _____

Exercise 16-4

MAGNA DATA, INC.
Income Statement
For Year Ended December 31, 2002

GENERAL JOURNAL   Page____

Date	Account Titles and Explanation	PR	Debit	Credit

SANBORN CORPORATION
Shareholders' Equity
October 31, 2002

Exercise 16-6

a.

GENERAL JOURNAL   Page____

Date	Account Titles and Explanation	PR	Debit	Credit

GENERAL JOURNAL   Page____

Date	Account Titles and Explanation	PR	Debit	Credit
b.				

c. **GENERAL JOURNAL**   Page____

Date	Account Titles and Explanation	PR	Debit	Credit

Exercise 16-7

FARGO INC.
Shareholders' Equity
December 31, 2002

Calculations:

Name _____

a. _____
_____
_____
_____
_____

b.

Time Period	Outstanding Shares	Effect of Share Split	Fraction of Year Outstanding	Weighted Average*

Round to the nearest whole share

Time Period	Outstanding Shares	Fraction of Year Outstanding	Weighted Average*

c. _____
_____
_____
_____
_____
_____

Exercise 16-16

a.

ALLAR CORPORATION
Statement of Retained Earnings
For Year Ended December 31, 2002

b.

ALLAR CORPORATION
Shareholders' Equity
December 31, 2002

Notes to Financial Statements:

_____

_____

_____

_____

_____

c.

_____

_____

_____

Exercise 16-17

_____

_____

_____

_____

_____

REDWARE COMPANY
Statement of Retained Earnings
For Year Ended December 31, 2002

*Exercise 16-19

AFFILIATED SYSTEMS, INC.
Shareholders' Equity
October 10, 2002

*Exercise 16-20

GENERAL JOURNAL   Page____

Date	Account Titles and Explanation	PR	Debit	Credit

Name
_____

GENERAL JOURNAL   Page____

Date	Account Titles and Explanation	PR	Debit	Credit

*Exercise 16-21

GENERAL JOURNAL   Page____

Date	Account Titles and Explanation	PR	Debit	Credit

Name _____

Part 1: Effect of income taxes (losses in parentheses)

Measure	Pre-Tax	30% Tax Effect	After-Tax

Part 2: Income from continuing operations:

Part 3: Income from discontinued operation:

Part 4: Income before extraordinary items:

Part 5: Net income:

Problem 16-2A

Part 1

a. 2000 weighted-average shares:

Time Period	Outstanding Shares	Effect of Share Dividend	Fraction of Year Outstanding	Weighted Average*

Round to the nearest whole share

b. 2001 weighted-average shares:

Time Period	Outstanding Shares	Fraction of Year Outstanding	Weighted Average*

Round to the nearest whole share

Name _____

c. 2002 weighted-average shares:

Time Period	Outstanding Shares	Effect of Share Split	Fraction of Year Outstanding	Weighted Average*

Round to the nearest whole share

Part 2
Earnings per share:

	(c) 2002	(b) 2001	(a) 2000

_____

_____

_____

_____

Problem 16-3A

1. _____

_____

_____

_____

_____

_____

_____

_____

_____

_____

2. _____

_____

_____

_____

_____

_____

_____

_____

Name _____

DAVIDSON INC.
Statement of Income and Retained Earnings
For Year Ended December 31, 2001

Chapter 16   Problem 16-1B   *Name* _____

Part 1: Effect of income taxes (losses in parentheses)

Measure	Pre-Tax	25% Tax Effect	After-Tax

Part 2: Income from continuing operations:

Part 3: Income from discontinued operation:

Part 4: Income before extraordinary items:

Part 5: Net income:

Problem 16-2B

Part 1

a. 2000 weighted-average shares:

Time Period	Outstanding Shares	Effect of Share Dividend	Fraction of Year Outstanding	Weighted Average*

Round to the nearest whole share

b. 2001 weighted-average shares:

Time Period	Outstanding Shares	Fraction of Year Outstanding	Weighted Average*

Round to the nearest whole share

Chapter 16   Problem 16-2B
(continued)

Name _____

c. 2002 weighted-average shares:

Time Period	Outstanding Shares	Effect of Share Split	Fraction of Year Outstanding	Weighted Average*

Round to the nearest whole share

Part 2
Earnings per share:

	(c) 2002	(b) 2001	(a) 2000

_____

Problem 16-3B

1. _____

2. _____

BOSWORTH INC.
Statement of Income and Retained Earnings
For Year Ended December 31, 2001

Part 1   Journal entries:

GENERAL JOURNAL   Page____

Date	Account Titles and Explanation	PR	Debit	Credit

Name

Part 2

CALDWELL CORP.
Statement of Retained Earnings
For Year Ended December 31, 2002

Part 3

CALDWELL CORP.
Shareholders' Equity
December 31, 2002

Problem 16-6B

Part 1

	Feb. 15	May 15	Aug. 15	Nov. 15

Name
_____

Part 2
Net income:

_____
_____
_____
_____
_____
_____
_____
_____
_____
_____
_____
_____
_____
_____
_____
_____
_____
_____

*Problem 16-7B

1. Journal entries:

GENERAL JOURNAL   Page____

Date	Account Titles and Explanation	PR	Debit	Credit

GENERAL JOURNAL   Page____

Date	Account Titles and Explanation	PR	Debit	Credit

Part 2

FRANCOIS CORP.
Statement of Retained Earnings
For Year Ended December 31, 2002

Part 3

FRANCOIS CORP.
Shareholders' Equity
December 31, 2002

Name _____

a. _____
b. _____
c. _____
d. _____

Quick Study 17-2

a. _____
b. _____

Quick Study 17-3

_____	serial bonds	_____	bearer bonds
_____	sinking fund bonds	_____	secured bonds
_____	convertible bonds	_____	debentures
_____	registered bonds	_____	bond indenture

Quick Study 17-4

a.   **GENERAL JOURNAL**   Page____

Date	Account Titles and Explanation	PR	Debit	Credit

b.   **GENERAL JOURNAL**   Page____

Date	Account Titles and Explanation	PR	Debit	Credit

Name _____

GENERAL JOURNAL

Page____

Date	Account Titles and Explanation	PR	Debit	Credit

Quick Study 17-6

	a.	b.	c.
PV of face amount			
PV of interest annuity			
Total issue price			

Calculations:

Quick Study 17-7

	a.	b.	c.
PV of face amount			
PV of interest annuity			
Total issue price			

Calculations:

Name _____

GENERAL JOURNAL   Page____

Date	Account Titles and Explanation	PR	Debit	Credit

Quick Study 17-9

GENERAL JOURNAL   Page____

Date	Account Titles and Explanation	PR	Debit	Credit

Quick Study 17-10

a.

_____
_____
_____
_____
_____

b.

_____
_____

Quick Study 17-11

a.

_____
_____
_____
_____
_____

b.

_____
_____

GENERAL JOURNAL   Page____

Date	Account Titles and Explanation	PR	Debit	Credit

Quick Study 17-13

GENERAL JOURNAL   Page____

Date	Account Titles and Explanation	PR	Debit	Credit

Quick Study 17-14

GENERAL JOURNAL   Page____

Date	Account Titles and Explanation	PR	Debit	Credit

Quick Study 17-15

GENERAL JOURNAL   Page____

Date	Account Titles and Explanation	PR	Debit	Credit

Name _____

GENERAL JOURNAL   Page____

Date	Account Titles and Explanation	PR	Debit	Credit

Quick Study 17-17

GENERAL JOURNAL   Page____

Date	Account Titles and Explanation	PR	Debit	Credit

Quick Study 17-18

GENERAL JOURNAL   Page____

Date	Account Titles and Explanation	PR	Debit	Credit

Name _____

GENERAL JOURNAL   Page____

Date	Account Titles and Explanation	PR	Debit	Credit

Quick Study 17-20

GENERAL JOURNAL   Page____

Date	Account Titles and Explanation	PR	Debit	Credit

Quick Study 17-21

GENERAL JOURNAL   Page____

Date	Account Titles and Explanation	PR	Debit	Credit

Quick Study 17-22

_____
_____
_____
_____
_____

Name _____

GENERAL JOURNAL   Page____

Date	Account Titles and Explanation	PR	Debit	Credit

Quick Study 17-24

GENERAL JOURNAL   Page____

Date	Account Titles and Explanation	PR	Debit	Credit

Quick Study 17-25

GENERAL JOURNAL   Page____

Date	Account Titles and Explanation	PR	Debit	Credit

Name _____

GENERAL JOURNAL   Page____

Date	Account Titles and Explanation	PR	Debit	Credit

Quick Study 17-27

GENERAL JOURNAL   Page____

Date	Account Titles and Explanation	PR	Debit	Credit

Quick Study 17-28

GENERAL JOURNAL   Page____

Date	Account Titles and Explanation	PR	Debit	Credit

GENERAL JOURNAL   Page____

Date	Account Titles and Explanation	PR	Debit	Credit

Quick Study 17-30

GENERAL JOURNAL   Page____

Date	Account Titles and Explanation	PR	Debit	Credit

Quick Study 17-31

GENERAL JOURNAL   Page____

Date	Account Titles and Explanation	PR	Debit	Credit

Name _____

GENERAL JOURNAL   Page____

Date	Account Titles and Explanation	PR	Debit	Credit	♣

Quick Study 17-33

a. _____

b. _____

c. _____

_____

Quick Study 17-34

	2002	2003	2004
Beginning balance.........			
Interest rate..............			
Interest expense..........			
Ending balance...........			

Name _____

a. _____

_____

b.   GENERAL JOURNAL   Page____

Date	Account Titles and Explanation	PR	Debit	Credit

Exercise 17-2

a. _____

_____

b.   GENERAL JOURNAL   Page____

Date	Account Titles and Explanation	PR	Debit	Credit

Name _____

a.

| | GENERAL JOURNAL | | | Page____ |

Date	Account Titles and Explanation	PR	Debit	Credit

b.

| | GENERAL JOURNAL | | | Page____ |

Date	Account Titles and Explanation	PR	Debit	Credit

c.

| | GENERAL JOURNAL | | | Page____ |

Date	Account Titles and Explanation	PR	Debit	Credit

d.

| | GENERAL JOURNAL | | | Page____ |

Date	Account Titles and Explanation	PR	Debit	Credit

Name _____

GENERAL JOURNAL   Page____

Date	Account Titles and Explanation	PR	Debit	Credit

Exercise 17-5

	a.	b.	c.
PV of face amount			
PV of interest annuity			
Total issue price			

Calculations:

Exercise 17-6

	a.	b.	c.
PV of face amount			
PV of interest annuity			
Total issue price			

Calculations:

a.

_____

_____

b.

_____

_____

c.

_____

_____

d.

PV of face amount .... _____

PV of interest annuity .... _____

Total issue price .... _____

Calculations:

e.

GENERAL JOURNAL   Page____

Date	Account Titles and Explanation	PR	Debit	Credit

Exercise 17-8

a. Discount =

_____

_____

b. Total interest expense over the life of the bonds:

_____

_____

_____

_____

_____

_____

c. Amortization table:

Period Ending	(a) Beginning Balance Prior (e)	(b) Debit Interest Expense	(c) Credit Discount on Bonds	(d) Credit Cash	(e) Ending Balance (a) + (c)
June. 30/02					
Dec. 31/02					
Jun. 30/03					
Dec. 31/03					
Jun. 30/04					
Dec. 31/04					
Total					

Exercise 17-9

a. Discount =

_____

_____

b. Total interest expense over the life of the bonds:

_____

_____

_____

_____

_____

c. Amortization table:

Period Ending	(a) Beginning Balance Prior (e)	(b) Debit Interest Expense	(c) Credit Discount on Bonds	(d) Credit Cash	(e) Ending Balance (a) + (c)
June. 30/02					
Dec. 31/02					
Jun. 30/03					
Dec. 31/03					
Jun. 30/04					
Dec. 31/04					
Total					

a.

_____
_____
_____
_____
_____
_____
_____

Amortization table:

Period Ending	(a) Beginning Balance Prior (e)	(b) Debit Interest Expense	(c) Credit Discount on Bonds	(d) Credit Cash	(e) Ending Balance (a) + (c)
Oct. 31/02					
Apr. 30/03					
Oct. 31/03					
Apr. 30/04					
Oct. 31/04					
Apr. 30/05					
Oct. 31/05					
Apr. 30/06					
Oct. 31/06					
Apr. 30/07					
Total					

b.   **GENERAL JOURNAL**   Page____

Date	Account Titles and Explanation	PR	Debit	Credit

Chapter 17   Exercise 17-11   *Name* _____

a.

PV of face amount .... _____

PV of interest annuity .... _____

Total issue price .... _____

Calculations:

b. Amortization table:

Period Ending	(a) Cash Interest Paid	(b) Period Interest Expense	(c) Discount Amort.	(d) Unamortized Discount	(e) Carrying Value
Oct. 1/02					
Oct. 1/03					
Oct. 1/04					
Oct. 1/05					
Oct. 1/06					
Oct. 1/07					
Oct. 1/08					
Oct. 1/09					
Total					

Calculations:

Exercise 17-12

1a.   **GENERAL JOURNAL**   Page____

Date	Account Titles and Explanation	PR	Debit	Credit

1b.   GENERAL JOURNAL   Page____

Date	Account Titles and Explanation	PR	Debit	Credit

1c.   GENERAL JOURNAL   Page____

Date	Account Titles and Explanation	PR	Debit	Credit

2.

_____

_____

_____

_____

Exercise 17-13

a.

PV of face amount .... _____

PV of interest annuity .... _____

Total issue price .... _____

Calculations:

b. Amortization table:

Period Ending	(a) Cash Interest Paid	(b) Period Interest Expense	(c) Discount Amort.	(d) Unamortized Discount	(e) Carrying Value
Oct. 1/02					
Oct. 1/03					
Oct. 1/04					
Oct. 1/05					
Oct. 1/06					
Oct. 1/07					
Oct. 1/08					
Oct. 1/09					
Total					

Calculations:

Exercise 17-14

a.   GENERAL JOURNAL   Page____

Date	Account Titles and Explanation	PR	Debit	Credit

b.   GENERAL JOURNAL   Page____

Date	Account Titles and Explanation	PR	Debit	Credit

c.

_____

_____

_____

_____

_____

Exercise 17-15

a.   GENERAL JOURNAL   Page____

Date	Account Titles and Explanation	PR	Debit	Credit

b.   GENERAL JOURNAL   Page____

Date	Account Titles and Explanation	PR	Debit	Credit

Exercise 17-16

a. _____

_____

b. _____

_____

c. _____

_____

d.

PV of face amount .... _____

PV of interest annuity .... _____

Total issue price .... _____

Calculations:

Chapter 17   Exercise 17-16
(continued)

Name
_____

e.

GENERAL JOURNAL   Page____

Date		Account Titles and Explanation	PR	Debit	Credit

Exercise 17-17

a. _____
_____

b. _____
_____
_____
_____
_____

c. Amortization table:

Period Ending	(a) Beginning Balance Prior (e)	(b) Debit Interest Expense	(c) Debit Premium on Bonds	(d) Credit Cash	(e) Ending Balance (a) - (c)
Jun. 30/02					
Dec. 31/02					
Jun. 30/03					
Dec. 31/03					
Jun. 30/04					
Dec. 31/04					
Total					

Exercise 17-18

a.
PV of face amount .... _____
PV of interest annuity .... _____
Total issue price .... _____

Calculations:

b. Amortization table:

Period Ending	(a) Cash Interest Paid	(b) Period Interest Expense	(c) Premium Amort.	(d) Unamortized Premium	(e) Carrying Value
Oct. 1/02					
Oct. 1/03					
Oct. 1/04					
Oct. 1/05					
Oct. 1/06					
Oct. 1/07					
Oct. 1/08					
Oct. 1/09					
Totals					

Calculations:

Exercise 17-19

1a.   GENERAL JOURNAL   Page____

Date	Account Titles and Explanation	PR	Debit	Credit

1b.   GENERAL JOURNAL   Page____

Date	Account Titles and Explanation	PR	Debit	Credit

1c.   GENERAL JOURNAL   Page____

Date	Account Titles and Explanation	PR	Debit	Credit

2.

_____

_____

_____

_____

Exercise 17-20

a.

PV of face amount .... _____

PV of interest annuity .... _____

Total issue price .... _____

Calculations:

b. Amortization table:

Period Ending	(a) Cash Interest Paid	(b) Period Interest Expense	(c) Premium Amort.	(d) Unamortized Premium	(e) Carrying Value
Oct. 1/02					
Oct. 1/03					
Oct. 1/04					
Oct. 1/05					
Oct. 1/06					
Oct. 1/07					
Oct. 1/08					
Oct. 1/09					
Totals					

Calculations:

1a.   GENERAL JOURNAL   Page____

Date	Account Titles and Explanation	PR	Debit	Credit

1b.   GENERAL JOURNAL   Page____

Date	Account Titles and Explanation	PR	Debit	Credit

1c.   GENERAL JOURNAL   Page____

Date	Account Titles and Explanation	PR	Debit	Credit

2.

_____

_____

_____

_____

Exercise 17-22

a. _____

b. _____

_____

c. _____

_____

_____

_____

d. _____
_____
_____
_____
_____
_____
_____
_____
_____
_____
_____

e. _____
_____
_____

f. _____
_____
_____
_____

g.   **GENERAL JOURNAL**   Page____

Date	Account Titles and Explanation	PR	Debit	Credit

Exercise 17-23

a. _____
_____

b. Amortization table:

Period Ending	(a) Beginning Balance Prior (e)	(b) Debit Interest Expense	(c) Debit Notes Payable	(d) Credit Cash (b) + (c)	(e) Ending Balance (a) − (c)
2003					
2004					
2005					
2006					
Totals					

Name _____

GENERAL JOURNAL

Page____

Date	Account Titles and Explanation	PR	Debit	Credit

Exercise 17-25

a. _____

b. Amortization table:

Period Ending	(a) Beginning Balance Prior (e)	(b) Debit Interest Expense	(c) Debit Notes Payable	(d) Credit Cash (b) + (c)	(e) Ending Balance (a) – (c)
2003					
2004					
2005					
2006					
Totals					

Name _____

GENERAL JOURNAL   Page____

Date	Account Titles and Explanation	PR	Debit	Credit

*Exercise 17-27

GENERAL JOURNAL   Page____

Date	Account Titles and Explanation	PR	Debit	Credit
a.				
b.				

GENERAL JOURNAL   Page____

Date	Account Titles and Explanation	PR	Debit	Credit
c.				
d.				

e.

(a) Year	(b) Beginning Net liability	(c) Payment	(d) Interest Expense (b) x 10%	(e) Reduction in lease liability (c) - (d)	(f) Lease Liability at End of Year (b) – (e)
2003					
2004					
2005					
2006					
2007					
Total					

Problem 17-1A

1a.
PV of face amount .... _____
PV of interest annuity .... _____
Total issue price .... _____

1b.   **GENERAL JOURNAL**   Page____

Date	Account Titles and Explanation	PR	Debit	Credit

Name _____

2a.
PV of face amount .... _____
PV of interest annuity .... _____
Total issue price .... _____

2b.   GENERAL JOURNAL   Page____

Date	Account Titles and Explanation	PR	Debit	Credit

3a.
PV of face amount .... _____
PV of interest annuity .... _____
Total issue price .... _____

3b.   GENERAL JOURNAL   Page____

Date	Account Titles and Explanation	PR	Debit	Credit

Problem 17-2A

1.   GENERAL JOURNAL   Page____

Date	Account Titles and Explanation	PR	Debit	Credit

2. _____
_____
_____
_____
_____
_____

3.

_____
_____
_____
_____
_____
_____

4.

Period Ending	Beginning Discount Balance	Amount Amortized	Ending Discount Balance
Jun. 30/02			
Dec. 31/02			
Jun. 30/03			
Dec. 31/03			

5. Amortization table:

Period Ending	(a) Beginning Balance Prior (e)	(b) Debit Interest Expense	(c) Credit Discount on Bonds	(d) Credit Cash (b) + (c)	(e) Ending Balance (a) + (c)
Jun. 30/02					
Dec. 31/02					
Jun. 30/03					
Dec. 31/03					

6.   GENERAL JOURNAL   Page____

Date	Account Titles and Explanation	PR	Debit	Credit

1.
PV of face amount .... _____
PV of interest annuity .... _____
Total issue price .... _____

2.   GENERAL JOURNAL   Page____

Date	Account Titles and Explanation	PR	Debit	Credit

3.

_____
_____
_____
_____
_____
_____
_____

4. Amortization table:

Period Ending	(a) Beginning Balance Prior (e)	(b) Debit Interest Expense	(c) Credit Discount on Bonds	(d) Credit Cash (b) + (c)	(e) Ending Balance (a) + (c)
Jun. 30/02					
Dec. 31/02					
Jun. 30/03					
Dec. 31/03					
Totals					

5.

Period Ending	Beginning Discount Balance	Amount Amortized	Ending Discount Balance
Jun. 30/02			
Dec. 31/02			
Jun. 30/03			
Dec. 31/03			

6.   GENERAL JOURNAL   Page____

Date	Account Titles and Explanation	PR	Debit	Credit

7.

_____

_____

_____

_____

_____

_____

_____

Problem 17-4A

a.

PV of face amount .... _____

PV of interest annuity .... _____

Total issue price .... _____

b. Amortization table:

	(a)	(b)	(c)	(d)	(e)
Period Ending	Cash Interest Paid	Period Interest Expense	Discount Amort.	Unamortized Discount	Carrying Value
Feb. 1/02					
May 1/02					
Aug. 1/02					
Nov. 1/02					
Feb. 1/03					
May 1/03					
Aug. 1/03					
Nov. 1/03					
Feb. 1/04					
May 1/04					
Aug. 1/04					
Nov. 1/04					
Feb. 1/05					
May 1/05					
Aug. 1/05					
Nov. 1/05					
Feb. 1/06					
Totals					

Calculations:

1a.   GENERAL JOURNAL   Page____

Date	Account Titles and Explanation	PR	Debit	Credit

1b.   GENERAL JOURNAL   Page____

Date	Account Titles and Explanation	PR	Debit	Credit

1c.   GENERAL JOURNAL   Page____

Date	Account Titles and Explanation	PR	Debit	Credit

1d.   GENERAL JOURNAL   Page____

Date	Account Titles and Explanation	PR	Debit	Credit

2.

_____

_____

_____

_____

a.

PV of face amount .... _____

PV of interest annuity .... _____

Total issue price .... _____

b. Amortization table:

	(a)	(b)	(c)	(d)	(e)
Period Ending	Cash Interest Paid	Period Interest Expense	Discount Amort.	Unamortized Discount	Carrying Value
June 1/02					
Dec. 1/02					
June 1/03					
Dec. 1/03					
June 1/04					
Dec. 1/04					
June 1/05					
Totals					

Calculations:

Problem 17-7A

1a.   **GENERAL JOURNAL**   Page____

Date	Account Titles and Explanation	PR	Debit	Credit

1b.   **GENERAL JOURNAL**   Page____

Date	Account Titles and Explanation	PR	Debit	Credit

Name

1c.   GENERAL JOURNAL   Page____

Date	Account Titles and Explanation	PR	Debit	Credit

1d.   GENERAL JOURNAL   Page____

Date	Account Titles and Explanation	PR	Debit	Credit

2.

_____

_____

_____

_____

Problem 17-8A

Part 1

_____

_____

_____

_____

_____

Name
_____

Part 2: Period Ending	(a) Beginning Balance Prior (e)	(b) Debit Interest Expense	(c) Debit Premium on Bonds	(d) Credit Cash	(e) Ending Balance (a) - (c)
Jun. 30/02					
Dec. 31/02					
Jun. 30/03					
Dec. 31/03					
Jun. 30/04					
Dec. 31/04					
Jun. 30/05					
Dec. 31/05					
Jun. 30/06					
Dec. 31/06					
Totals					

3.   **GENERAL JOURNAL**   Page____

Date	Account Titles and Explanation	PR	Debit	Credit

4.
PV of face amount .... _____
PV of interest annuity .... _____
Total issue price .... _____

Problem 17-9A

Bond Issue A:
a. _____

b.   **GENERAL JOURNAL**   Page____

Date	Account Titles and Explanation	PR	Debit	Credit

Name

c. _____

d. _____

e. _____

f. _____

g. _____
_____
_____
_____
_____

h. _____
_____
_____
_____

i.

GENERAL JOURNAL   Page____

Date	Account Titles and Explanation	PR	Debit	Credit

Bond Issue B:

a. _____

b.

GENERAL JOURNAL   Page____

Date	Account Titles and Explanation	PR	Debit	Credit

Name

_____

c. _____

d. _____

e. _____

f. _____

g. _____

_____

_____

_____

_____

h. _____

_____

_____

_____

i.   **GENERAL JOURNAL**   Page____

Date	Account Titles and Explanation	PR	Debit	Credit

Problem 17-10A

Part 1

_____

_____

_____

_____

_____

_____

_____

Part 2

Period Ending	(a) Beginning Balance Prior (e)	(b) Debit Interest Expense	(c) Debit Notes Payable (d) – (b)	(d) Credit Cash (b) + (c)	(e) Ending Balance (a) - (c)
Nov. 30/03					
Nov. 30/04					
Nov. 30/05					
Nov. 30/06					
Totals					

3.   GENERAL JOURNAL   Page____

Date	Account Titles and Explanation	PR	Debit	Credit

Part 4

Period Ending	(a) Beginning Balance Prior (e)	(b) Debit Interest Expense	(c) Debit Notes Payable (d) – (b)	(d) Credit Cash (b) + (c)	(e) Ending Balance (a) - (c)
Nov. 30/03					
Nov. 30/04					
Nov. 30/05					
Nov. 30/06					
Totals					

GENERAL JOURNAL   Page____

Date	Account Titles and Explanation	PR	Debit	Credit

*Problem 17-11A

Part 1
_____

_____

Part 2

(a) Year	(b) Beginning Net liability	(c) Payment	(d) Interest Expense	(e) Reduction in lease liability (c) - (d)	(f) Lease Liability at End of Year (b) – (e)
2001					
2002					
2003					
2004					
Total					

Part 3   GENERAL JOURNAL   Page____

Date	Account Titles and Explanation	PR	Debit	Credit

Part 4   GENERAL JOURNAL   Page____

Date	Account Titles and Explanation	PR	Debit	Credit

GENERAL JOURNAL   Page____

Date	Account Titles and Explanation	PR	Debit	Credit

WESON ENGINEERING COMPANY
Balance Sheet
December 31, 2002

Part 5   ## GENERAL JOURNAL   Page____

Date	Account Titles and Explanation	PR	Debit	Credit

6. GENERAL JOURNAL Page____

Date	Account Titles and Explanation	PR	Debit	Credit

Problem 17-1B

1a.
PV of face amount .... _____
PV of interest annuity .... _____
Total issue price .... _____

1b. GENERAL JOURNAL Page____

Date	Account Titles and Explanation	PR	Debit	Credit

2a.
PV of face amount .... _____
PV of interest annuity .... _____
Total issue price .... _____

2b. GENERAL JOURNAL Page____

Date	Account Titles and Explanation	PR	Debit	Credit

3a.
PV of face amount .... _____
PV of interest annuity .... _____
Total issue price .... _____

3b.   GENERAL JOURNAL   Page____

Date	Account Titles and Explanation	PR	Debit	Credit

Problem 17-2B

1a.
PV of face amount .... _____
PV of interest annuity .... _____
Total issue price .... _____

1b.   GENERAL JOURNAL   Page____

Date	Account Titles and Explanation	PR	Debit	Credit

2.
_____
_____
_____
_____
_____
_____

Name _____

3.

_____
_____
_____
_____
_____
_____

4. Amortization table:

Period Ending	(a) Beginning Balance Prior (e)	(b) Debit Interest Expense	(c) Credit Premium on Bonds	(d) Credit Cash (b) + (c)	(e) Ending Balance (a) - (c)
Jun. 30/02					
Dec. 31/02					

5.   GENERAL JOURNAL   Page____

Date	Account Titles and Explanation	PR	Debit	Credit

6.

Period Ending	Beginning Premium Balance	Amount Amortized	Ending Premium Balance
Jun. 30/02			
Dec. 31/02			
Jun. 30/03			
Dec. 31/03			

1.
PV of face amount .... _____
PV of interest annuity .... _____
Total issue price .... _____

GENERAL JOURNAL   Page____

Date	Account Titles and Explanation	PR	Debit	Credit

2.

_____
_____
_____
_____
_____
_____
_____

3. Amortization table:

Period Ending	(a) Beginning Carrying Amount	(b) Interest Expense for the Period	(c) Interest to be Paid to Bondholders	(d) Discount to be Amortized	(e) Ending Carrying Amount
Jun. 30/02					
Dec. 31/02					

4.   ### GENERAL JOURNAL   Page____

Date	Account Titles and Explanation	PR	Debit	Credit

a.
PV of face amount .... _____

PV of interest annuity .... _____

Total issue price .... _____

b. Amortization table:

Period Ending	(a) Cash Interest Paid	(b) Period Interest Expense	(c) Premium Amort.	(d) Unamortized Premium	(e) Carrying Value
May 1/02					
Aug. 1/02					
Nov. 1/02					
Feb. 1/03					
May 1/03					
Aug. 1/03					
Nov. 1/03					
Feb. 1/04					
May 1/04					
Aug. 1/04					
Nov. 1/04					
Feb. 1/05					
May 1/05					
Totals					

Calculations:

Name

1a.   GENERAL JOURNAL   Page____

Date		Account Titles and Explanation	PR	Debit	Credit

1b.   GENERAL JOURNAL   Page____

Date		Account Titles and Explanation	PR	Debit	Credit

1c.   GENERAL JOURNAL   Page____

Date		Account Titles and Explanation	PR	Debit	Credit

1d.   GENERAL JOURNAL   Page____

Date		Account Titles and Explanation	PR	Debit	Credit

2.

_____

_____

_____

_____

Fundamental Accounting Principles, 10th Canadian Edition

a.
PV of face amount .... _____
PV of interest annuity .... _____
Total issue price .... _____

b. Amortization table:

Period Ending	(a) Cash Interest Paid	(b) Period Interest Expense	(c) Premium Amort.	(d) Unamortized Premium	(e) Carrying Value
Sept. 1/02					
Mar. 1/03					
Sept. 1/03					
Mar. 1/04					
Sept. 1/04					
Mar. 1/05					
Sept. 1/05					
Mar. 1/06					
Sept. 1/06					
Totals					

Calculations:

Problem 17-7B

1a.   GENERAL JOURNAL   Page____

Date	Account Titles and Explanation	PR	Debit	Credit

1b.   GENERAL JOURNAL   Page____

Date	Account Titles and Explanation	PR	Debit	Credit

© 2002 McGraw-Hill Ryerson Limited.

1c.   GENERAL JOURNAL   Page____

Date	Account Titles and Explanation	PR	Debit	Credit

1d.   GENERAL JOURNAL   Page____

Date	Account Titles and Explanation	PR	Debit	Credit

2.

_____

_____

_____

_____

Problem 17-8B

Part 1

_____

_____

_____

_____

_____

Name _____

Period Ending	(a) Cash Interest Paid	(b) Bond Interest Expense	(c) Premium Amortization	(d) Unamortized Premium	(e) Carrying Value
Jan. 01/02					
June 30/02					
Dec. 31/02					
June 30/03					
Dec. 31/03					
June 30/04					
Dec. 31/04					
June 30/05					
Dec. 31/05					
June 30/06					
Dec. 31/06					
Totals					

3.   GENERAL JOURNAL   Page____

Date	Account Titles and Explanation	PR	Debit	Credit

4.
PV of face amount .... _____
PV of interest annuity .... _____
Total issue price .... _____

Problem 17-9B

Bond Issue 1:
a. _____

b.   GENERAL JOURNAL   Page____

Date	Account Titles and Explanation	PR	Debit	Credit

c. _____

d. _____

e. _____

f. _____

g. _____

_____

_____

_____

h. _____

_____

_____

_____

i.   **GENERAL JOURNAL**   Page____

Date	Account Titles and Explanation	PR	Debit	Credit

Bond Issue 2:

a. _____

b.   **GENERAL JOURNAL**   Page____

Date	Account Titles and Explanation	PR	Debit	Credit

c. _____

d. _____

e. _____

f. _____

g. _____

_____

_____

_____

h. _____

_____

_____

_____

i.   **GENERAL JOURNAL**   Page____

Date	Account Titles and Explanation	PR	Debit	Credit

Problem 17-10B

Part 1

_____

_____

_____

_____

_____

_____

_____

_____

Part 2

Period Ending	(a) Beginning Balance Prior (e)	(b) Periodic Payment	(c) Interest Expense for the Period	(d) Portion of Payment that is Principal	(e) Ending Balance (a) - (d)
Nov. 30/02					
Apr. 30/03					
Nov. 30/03					
Apr. 30/04					
Nov. 30/04					
Apr. 30/05					
Nov. 30/05					
Apr. 30/06					
Totals					

3.

GENERAL JOURNAL   Page____

Date	Account Titles and Explanation	PR	Debit	Credit

Part 4

Period Ending	(a) Beginning Balance	(b) Debit Interest Expense	(c) Debit Notes Payable (d) – (b)	(d) Credit Cash (b) + (c)	(e) Ending Balance (a) - (c)
Nov. 30/02					
Apr. 30/03					
Nov. 30/03					
Apr. 30/04					
Nov. 30/04					
Apr. 30/05					
Nov. 30/05					
Apr. 30/06					
Totals					

Name _____

GENERAL JOURNAL   Page____

Date	Account Titles and Explanation	PR	Debit	Credit

*Problem 17-11B

Part 1 _____

_____

Part 2

(a) Year	(b) Beginning Net liability	(c) Payment	(d) Interest Expense (b) x 12%	(e) Reduction in lease liability (c) - (d)	(f) Lease Liability at End of Year (b) – (e)
2001					
2002					
2003					
2004					
2005					
2006					
Total					

Part 3   GENERAL JOURNAL   Page____

Date	Account Titles and Explanation	PR	Debit	Credit

Part 4   GENERAL JOURNAL   Page____

Date	Account Titles and Explanation	PR	Debit	Credit

STONEY POINT SERVICES COMPANY
Balance Sheet
December 31, 2002

Part 5   GENERAL JOURNAL   Page____

Date	Account Titles and Explanation	PR	Debit	Credit

6.   GENERAL JOURNAL   Page____

Date	Account Titles and Explanation	PR	Debit	Credit

Name _____

(1) _____
(2) _____
(3) _____
(4) _____
(5) _____

Quick Study 18-2

_____
_____
_____

Quick Study 18-3

_____
_____
_____
_____

Quick Study 18-4

GENERAL JOURNAL

Date	Account Titles and Explanation	Post Ref.	Debit	Credit

GENERAL JOURNAL

Date	Account Titles and Explanation	Post Ref.	Debit	Credit

Quick Study 18-6

GENERAL JOURNAL

Date	Account Titles and Explanation	Post Ref.	Debit	Credit

Quick Study 18-7

GENERAL JOURNAL

Date	Account Titles and Explanation	Post Ref.	Debit	Credit

© 2002 McGraw-Hill Ryerson Limited.

GENERAL JOURNAL

Date	Account Titles and Explanation	Post Ref.	Debit	Credit

Quick Study 18-9

_____

_____

_____

Quick Study 18-10

GENERAL JOURNAL

Date	Account Titles and Explanation	Post Ref.	Debit	Credit

GENERAL JOURNAL

Date	Account Titles and Explanation	Post Ref.	Debit	Credit

Quick Study 18-12

GENERAL JOURNAL

Date	Account Titles and Explanation	Post Ref.	Debit	Credit

GENERAL JOURNAL

Date	Account Titles and Explanation	Post Ref.	Debit	Credit

GENERAL JOURNAL

Date	Account Titles and Explanation	Post Ref.	Debit	Credit

_____
_____
_____
_____
_____
_____
_____
_____
_____
_____
_____

GENERAL JOURNAL

Date	Account Titles and Explanation	Post Ref.	Debit	Credit

Exercise 18-4

_____
_____
_____
_____
_____
_____
_____
_____
_____
_____
_____

Exercise 18-5

GENERAL JOURNAL

Date	Account Titles and Explanation	Post Ref.	Debit	Credit

Exercise 18-6

GENERAL JOURNAL

Date	Account Titles and Explanation	Post Ref.	Debit	Credit

GENERAL JOURNAL

Date	Account Titles and Explanation	Post Ref.	Debit	Credit

Supporting Computations:

Name _____

(a)

(b)

(c)

(d)

(e)

GENERAL JOURNAL

Date	Account Titles and Explanation	Post Ref.	Debit	Credit

Exercise 18-10

GENERAL JOURNAL

Date	Account Titles and Explanation	Post Ref.	Debit	Credit

Name _____

GENERAL JOURNAL

Date	Account Titles and Explanation	Post Ref.	Debit	Credit

Exercise 18-12

_____

_____

_____

_____

_____

GENERAL JOURNAL

Date	Account Titles and Explanation	Post Ref.	Debit	Credit

GENERAL JOURNAL

Date	Account Titles and Explanation	Post Ref.	Debit	Credit

Book value _____

_____

_____

_____

_____

_____

_____

_____

_____

_____

_____

Exercise 18-13

_____

_____

_____

_____

_____

_____

_____

_____

_____

_____

Name _____

Name _____

GENERAL JOURNAL

Date	Account Titles and Explanation	Post Ref.	Debit	Credit

Fundamental Accounting Principles, 10th Canadian Edition

GENERAL JOURNAL

Date	Account Titles and Explanation	Post Ref.	Debit	Credit

Part 1
(1)

GENERAL JOURNAL

Date	Account Titles and Explanation	Post Ref.	Debit	Credit
2002:				
:				
:				

Name _____

GENERAL JOURNAL

Date	Account Titles and Explanation	Post Ref.	Debit	Credit
2002:				
:				
:				

Part 2

_____
_____
_____
_____
_____
_____
_____
_____
_____
_____
_____

GENERAL JOURNAL

Date	Account Titles and Explanation	Post Ref.	Debit	Credit
2002				

Problem 18-3A

GENERAL JOURNAL

Date	Account Titles and Explanation	Post Ref.	Debit	Credit

Name _____

_____

_____

_____

_____

_____

_____

_____

_____

_____

_____

_____

_____

_____

_____

_____

_____

_____

Part 2

GENERAL JOURNAL

Date	Account Titles and Explanation	Post Ref.	Debit	Credit

Part 3

_____

_____

_____

_____

_____

_____

_____

_____

_____

_____

Name _____

GENERAL JOURNAL

Date	Account Titles and Explanation	Post Ref.	Debit	Credit
2000				
2001				

_____

_____

_____

_____

_____

_____

_____

_____

_____

_____

_____

_____

_____

_____

Part 2

GENERAL JOURNAL

Date	Account Titles and Explanation	Post Ref.	Debit	Credit
2000				
2001				

_____
_____
_____
_____
_____
_____
_____
_____
_____
_____
_____
_____
_____
_____
_____

Problem 18-6A
Part 1

GENERAL JOURNAL

Date	Account Titles and Explanation	Post Ref.	Debit	Credit

Name _____

GENERAL JOURNAL

Date	Account Titles and Explanation	Post Ref.	Debit	Credit

Part 2

_____
_____
_____
_____
_____
_____
_____
_____
_____

_____
_____
_____
_____
_____
_____
_____
_____
_____
_____
_____
_____
_____
_____
_____
_____
_____
_____
_____
_____
_____

Problem 18-7A

GENERAL JOURNAL

Date	Account Titles and Explanation	Post Ref.	Debit	Credit

Part 2

Northwood Company and Souther Company
Worksheet for Consolidated balance Sheet
As of December 31, 2001

	Northwood	Souther	Eliminations		Consolidated
			Debit	Credit	
Cash					
Notes receivable					
Merchandise					
Building-net					
Land					
Investment in Souther					
Excess of cost over book value					
Accounts payable					
Note payable					
Common shares, Northwood					
Retained Earnings, Northwood					
Common Shares, Souther					
Retained Earnings, Souther					
Minority Interest					

Name _____

GENERAL JOURNAL

Date	Account Titles and Explanation	Post Ref.	Debit	Credit

Part 1
(1)

GENERAL JOURNAL

Date	Account Titles and Explanation	Post Ref.	Debit	Credit
2002:				
:				
:				

GENERAL JOURNAL

Date	Account Titles and Explanation	Post Ref.	Debit	Credit
2002:				
:				
:				

Part 2

_____

_____

_____

_____

_____

_____

_____

_____

_____

_____

GENERAL JOURNAL

Date	Account Titles and Explanation	Post Ref.	Debit	Credit
2002				

Problem 18-3B

GENERAL JOURNAL

Date	Account Titles and Explanation	Post Ref.	Debit	Credit

Name _____

_____
_____
_____
_____
_____
_____
_____
_____
_____
_____
_____
_____
_____
_____
_____
_____
_____
_____

Part 2

GENERAL JOURNAL

Date	Account Titles and Explanation	Post Ref.	Debit	Credit

Part 3

_____
_____
_____
_____
_____
_____
_____
_____
_____

© 2002 McGraw-Hill Ryerson Limited.

Name _____

GENERAL JOURNAL

Date	Account Titles and Explanation	Post Ref.	Debit	Credit
2001				
2002				
2003				

(2) _____
_____
_____
_____

(3) _____
_____
_____
_____
_____
_____
_____
_____
_____

Part 2

GENERAL JOURNAL

Date	Account Titles and Explanation	Post Ref.	Debit	Credit
2001				
2002				

GENERAL JOURNAL

Date	Account Titles and Explanation	Post Ref.	Debit	Credit
2003				

(2) _____
_____
_____
_____
_____

(3) _____
_____
_____
_____
_____
_____
_____
_____
_____

GENERAL JOURNAL

Date	Account Titles and Explanation	Post Ref.	Debit	Credit

_____
_____
_____
_____
_____
_____
_____
_____
_____

Part 3

_____
_____
_____
_____
_____
_____
_____
_____
_____
_____
_____
_____
_____
_____
_____
_____
_____

Part 1

Name

Part 2

Name _____

Northwood Company and Souther Company
Worksheet for Consolidated balance Sheet
As of December 31, 2001

	Northwood	Souther	Eliminations		Consolidated
			Debit	Credit	
Cash					
Notes receivable					
Merchandise					
Building-net					
Land					
Investment in Souther					
Excess of cost over book value					
Accounts payable					
Note payable					
Common shares, Northwood					
Retained Earnings, Northwood					
Common Shares, Souther					
Retained Earnings, Souther					
Minority Interest					

A&R Problem 18-2

(a)

GENERAL JOURNAL

Date	Account Titles and Explanation	Post Ref.	Debit	Credit

GENERAL JOURNAL

Date	Account Titles and Explanation	Post Ref.	Debit	Credit

Name _____

_____
_____
_____
_____
_____
_____

Quick Study 19-2

(1) _____   (6) _____
(2) _____   (7) _____
(3) _____   (8) _____
(4) _____   (9) _____
(5) _____   (10) _____

Quick Study 19-3

(1) _____   (6) _____
(2) _____   (7) _____
(3) _____   (8) _____
(4) _____
(5) _____

Quick Study 19-4

Fundamental Accounting Principles, 10th Canadian Edition

(1) _____
_____

(2) _____
_____

(3) _____
_____

(4) _____
_____

(5) _____
_____

(6) _____
_____
_____

Chapter 19   Quick Study 19-5   *Name* _____

(1) _____

(2) _____

(3) _____
_____

Quick Study 19-6

_____
_____
_____
_____
_____

Quick Study 19-7

_____
_____
_____
_____
_____
_____

Quick Study 19-8

Quick Study 19-10

Quick Study 19-11[A]

Quick Study 19-13

Quick Study 19-14

Quick Study 19-16

Quick Study 19-17

Name _____

	Statement of Cash Flows			Footnote Describing Noncash Investing & Financing Activities	Not Reported on Statement or in Footnote
	Operating Activities	_Investing Activities_	_Financing Activities_		
a. Long-term bonds payable were retired by issuing common shares.					
b. Surplus merchandise inventory was sold for cash.					
c. Borrowed cash from the bank by signing a nine-month note payable.					
d. Paid cash to purchase a patent.					
e. A six-month note receivable was accepted in exchange for a building that had been used in operations.					
f. Recorded amortization expense on all plant assets.					
g. A cash dividend that had been declared in a previous period was paid in the current period.					

Burton COMPANY
Statement of Cash Flows
For Year Ended December 31, 2002

Case A

Case B

Case C

Name _____

Case A

Case B

Case C .

Exercise 19-6

Exercise 19-8

	Statement of Cash Flows			Footnote Describing Noncash Investing & Financing Activities	Not Reported on Statement or in Footnote
	Operating Activities	Investing Activities	Financing Activities		
a. Land for a new plant is purchased by issuing common shares.					
b. Recorded amortization expense.					
c. Income taxes payable increased by 15% from prior year.					
d. Declared and paid a cash dividend.					
e. Paid cash to purchase merchandise.					
f. Sold capital equipment at a loss.					
g. Accounts receivable decreased during the year.					

Name _____

YUKI CORPORATION
Statement of Cash Flows
For Year Ended December 31, 2000

Part 2

(1) _____

(2) _____

(3) _____

(4) _____

_____

Part 1
Notes:

(1) _____

_____

_____

_____

_____

(2) _____

_____

_____

_____

(3) _____

_____

_____

_____

(4) _____

_____

_____

_____

(5) _____

_____

_____

_____

_____

_____

_____

(6) _____

_____

_____

_____

_____

(7) _____

_____

_____

_____

_____

_____

Cormier Ltd.
Statement of Cash Flows (Direct Method)
For Year Ended June 30, 2002

Part 2

_____

_____

Exercise 19-13

	Adjust by	
Income Element	*Adding*	*Subtracting*
1. Changes in current assets:		
a. Increases	_____	_____
b. Decreases	_____	_____
2. Changes in current liabilities:		
a. Increases	_____	_____
b. Decreases	_____	_____
3. Amortization of capital assets	_____	_____
4. Amortization of intangible assets	_____	_____
5. Interest expense:		
a. Bond Premium amortized	_____	_____
b. Bond Discount amortized	_____	_____
6. Sale of non-current asset:		
a. Gain	_____	_____
b. Loss	_____	_____

Name _____

	Statement of Cash Flows					
	For Year Ended December 31, 2002					

Notes (supporting calculations):

| | Statement of Cash Flows | | | | | | |
	For Year Ended December 31, 2002						

Notes (supporting calculations):

Fundamental Accounting Principles, 10th Canadian Edition

Name

Statement of Cash Flows
For Year Ended December 31, 2002

Name _____

Statement of Cash Flows
For Year Ended December 31, 2002

Notes:

_____
_____
_____
_____
_____
_____
_____
_____
_____
_____

Statement of Cash Flows
For Year Ended December 31, 2002

Notes (supporting calculations):

Name _____

Spreadsheet for Statement of Cash Flows			
For Year Ended December 31, 2002			

Analysis of Changes

	December 31, 2001	*Debit*	*Credit*	December 31, 2002
Balance sheet—debits:				
Cash...................................				
Accounts receivable......................				
Merchandise inventory..................				
Equipment..............................				
Balance sheet—credits:				
Accum. Amortization, equip...........				
Accounts payable				
Income taxes payable.....................				
Common shares, no par value.......				
Retained earnings				
Statement of cash flows:				
Operating activities:				
Net income................................				
Increase in accts. receivable				
Increase in merch. inventory..........				
Decrease in accounts payable.......				
Increase in income taxes payable .				
Amortization expense.....................				
Investing activities:				
Payment for equipment..................				
Financing activities:				
Issued common shares for cash...				
Paid cash dividends........................				

Name _____

	Spreadsheet for Statement of Cash Flows
	For Year Ended December 31, 2002

Analysis of Changes

	December 31, 2001	Debit	Credit	December 31, 2002
Balance sheet—debits:				
Cash.................................				
Accounts receivable				
Merchandise inventory....................				
Prepaid expenses...........................				
Equipment				
Balance sheet—credits:				
Accum. amortization, equip............				
Accounts payable				
Short-term notes payable				
Long-term notes payable................				
Common shares, no par value.......				
Retained earnings				
Statement of cash flows:				
Operating activities:				
Net income..................................				
Increase in accts. receivable				
Increase in merch. inventory..........				
Decrease in prepaid expenses.......				
Decrease in accounts payable.......				
Amortization expense.....................				
Loss on sale of equipment				
Investing activities:				
Receipt from sale of equipment.....				
Payment to purchase equipment ..				
Financing activities:				
Borrowed on short-term note.........				
Payment on long-term note............				
Issued common shares for cash ...				
Payments of cash dividends				
Noncash investing and financing activities:				
Purchase of equip. financed by long-term note payable........				

Statement of Cash Flows
For Year Ended December 31, 2002

Notes (supporting calculations):

Name _____

Statement of Cash Flows
For Year Ended December 31, 2002

Notes (supporting calculations):

Fundamental Accounting Principles, 10th Canadian Edition

Statement of Cash Flows
For Year Ended December 31, 2002

Name _____

Spreadsheet for Statement of Cash Flows
For Year Ended December 31, 2002

	December 31, 2001	Analysis of Changes		December 31, 2002
		Debit	Credit	
Balance sheet—debits:				
Cash..				
Accounts receivable				
Merchandise inventory....................				
Equipment				
Balance sheet—credits:				
Accum. Amortization, equip.				
Accounts payable				
Income taxes payable.....................				
Common shares, no par value.......				
Retained earnings				
Statement of cash flows:				
Operating activities:				
Net income.....................................				
Increase in accts. receivable				
Increase in merch. inventory..........				
Decrease in accounts payable.......				
Increase in income taxes payable .				
Amortization expense......................				
Investing activities:				
Payment for equipment...................				
Financing activities:				
Issued common shares for cash...				
Paid cash dividends........................				

Name _____

Statement of Cash Flows
For Year Ended December 31, 2002

Notes:

_____

_____

_____

_____

_____

_____

_____

_____

_____

Name _____

Statement of Cash Flows
For Year Ended December 31, 2002

Notes (supporting calculations):

Spreadsheet for Statement of Cash Flows
For Year Ended December 31, 2002

	December 31, 2001	Analysis of Changes		December 31, 2002
		Debit	Credit	
Balance sheet–debits:				
Cash..				
Accounts receivable				
Merchandise inventory....................				
Prepaid expenses..........................				
Equipment				
Balance sheet–credits:				
Accum. amortization, equip............				
Accounts payable				
Short-term notes payable				
Long-term notes payable				
Common shares, no par value.......				
Retained earnings				
Statement of cash flows:				
Operating activities:				
Net income................................				
Increase in accts. receivable				
Increase in merch. inventory				
Decrease in prepaid expenses.......				
Decrease in accounts payable.......				
Amortization expense....................				
Loss on sale of equipment				
Investing activities:				
Receipt from sale of equipment.....				
Payment to purchase equipment ..				
Financing activities:				
Borrowed on short-term note.........				
Payment on long-term note............				
Issued common shares for cash...				
Payments of cash dividends				
Noncash investing and financing activities:				
Purchase of equip. financed by long-term note payable........				

Name _____

Part 1

_____

Part 2

_____
_____
_____
_____
_____
_____
_____
_____
_____
_____

Part 4

_____
_____
_____
_____
_____
_____
_____
_____
_____
_____
_____
_____
_____
_____
_____
_____

Part 5

_____
_____
_____
_____
_____
_____
_____

Name _____

A&R Problem 19-2

(1) _____

(2) _____

(3) _____

(4) _____

(5) _____

(6) _____

(7) _____

(8) _____

(9) _____

_____

_____

(10) _____

_____

_____

A&R Problem 19-3

Statement of Cash Flows							
For Year Ended December 31, 2002							

Name _____

_____

Working Paper for Statement of Changes in Financial Position
For Year Ended December 31, 2002

Analysis of Changes

	December 31, 2001	Debit	Credit	December 31, 2002
Balance sheet–debits:				
Cash and cash equivalents				
Accounts receivable				
Merchandise inventory				
Prepaid expenses				
Icahn Corporation shares				
Land				
Buildings				
Equipment				
Balance sheet—credits:				
Accum. amortization, buildings.				
Accum. amortization, equip...........				
Notes payable				
Accounts payable				
Other accrued liabilities				
Interest payable				
Taxes payable				
Bonds payable				
Common shares				
Retained earnings				
Statement of changes in financial position:				
Operating activities:				
Net income				
Increase in accts. Receivable				
Increase in merch. Inventory				
Increase in prepaid expenses				
Decrease in accounts payable				
Amortization expense, bldg				
Amortization expense, equip				
Loss on sale of equipment				
Investing activities:				
Proceeds from sale of Icahn shares				
Purchase of land				

Name _____

Cash paid for equipment ....
Proceeds from sale of equipment ...
Financing activities:
Issue of note payable ....
Payment of notes payable ....
Proceeds from sale of bonds ....
Proceeds from sale of shares ....
Dividends paid ....
Increase in cash ....

Statement of Cash Flows
For Year Ended December 31, 2002

_____
_____
_____
_____
_____
_____

Quick Study 20-2

(a) _____
_____

(b) _____
_____
_____

Quick Study 20-3

_____
_____
_____
_____
_____
_____

Name _____

(a) _____
_____

(b) _____
_____

(c) _____
_____

Quick Study 20-5

(1) _____

_____

(2) _____

_____

(3) _____

_____

(4) _____

_____

(5) _____

_____

_____

Quick Study 20-7

.	6.
.	7.
.	8.
.	9.
.	0.

Quick Study 20-8

_____

_____

_____

_____

_____

_____

_____

_____

_____

_____

_____

_____

_____

_____
_____
_____
_____
_____
_____
_____
_____
_____
_____
_____
_____
_____
_____
_____
_____
_____
_____
_____
_____
_____
_____
_____
_____
_____

Quick Study 20-10

Ratio	2002	2001	Trend
1. Profit Margin	8%	9%	
2. Debt Ratio	35%	40%	
3. Gross Margin	33%	45%	
4. Acid-test Ratio	.99	1.10	
5. Accounts Receivable Turnover	6.4	5.6	
6. Basic Earnings Per Share	$1.18	$1.20	
7. Merchandise Turnover	3.5	3.3	
8. Dividend Yield	1%	.8%	

Name _____

_____
_____
_____
_____
_____
_____

Quick Study 20-12

_____
_____
_____
_____
_____
_____

Exercise 20-1

_____
_____
_____
_____
_____
_____
_____
_____
_____
_____
_____
_____

Name _____

_____
_____
_____
_____
_____
_____
_____
_____

Exercise 20-3

_____
_____
_____
_____
_____
_____
_____
_____
_____
_____
_____
_____
_____
_____

Carmon Company			
Common-Size Comparative Balance Sheet			
December 31, 2000-2002			
	2002	2001*	2000*

Exercise 20-5

(a) Current Ratio

2002: _____

_____

2001: _____

_____

2000: _____

_____

_____

Name _____

(b) Acid-test ratio
2002: _____

_____

_____

2001: _____

_____

_____

2000: _____

_____

_____

Analysis: _____

_____

_____

_____

_____

_____

_____

Exercise 20-6

	Case X	Case Y	Case Z
Current assets			
Current liabilities			
Current ratio			
Cash			
Temporary investments			
Accounts receivable			
Quick assets			
Current liabilities			
Acid-test ratio			

_____

_____

_____

_____

_____

Name _____

a.   Days' sales uncollected:
2002 _____
_____
_____
_____

2001 _____
_____
_____
_____

b.   Accounts receivable turnover:
2002 _____
_____
_____

2001: _____
_____
_____
_____

c.   Merchandise turnover:
2002 _____
_____
_____

2001 _____
_____
_____
_____

d.   Days' sales in inventory:
2002 _____
_____
_____

2001 _____
_____
_____
_____

Analysis: _____

_____

_____

_____

_____

_____

_____

_____

Exercise 20-8

Days' sales uncollected: _____

_____

_____

_____

_____

_____

_____

_____

Exercise 20-9

Accounts Receivable Turnover: _____

_____

_____

_____

_____

_____

_____

2. _____

_____

3. _____

_____

_____

© *2002 McGraw-Hill Ryerson Limited.*

Days sales in receivables

	2002	2001

Analysis:

_____
_____
_____
_____
_____
_____
_____
_____
_____
_____
_____
_____
_____

Exercise 20-11

Inventory turnovers:

	2002	2001

Analysis: _____

_____

_____

_____

_____

_____

_____

_____

_____

_____

_____

Exercise 20-12

Days sales in receivables

	2002	2001

Analysis: _____

_____

_____

_____

_____

_____

_____

_____

_____

_____

_____

_____
_____
_____
_____
_____
_____
_____
_____
_____
_____
_____
_____
_____
_____
_____
_____
_____
_____
_____
_____
_____
_____
_____

Exercise 20-14

Ration of pledged assets to secured liabilities:

	Grant Co.	Singh Co.
Pledged assets		
Secured liabilities		
Ratio		

Analysis:

_____
_____
_____
_____
_____
_____
_____

a.   Debt and equity ratios:

	2002	2001

b.   Pledged assets to secured liabilities:

2002: _____

2001: _____

c.   Times interest earned:

2002: _____

2001: _____

Analysis:

_____

_____

_____

_____

_____

_____

_____

_____

_____

_____

_____

_____

a.   Profit margin:

2002: _____

_____

_____

2001: _____

_____

_____

_____

b.   Total asset turnover:

2002: _____

_____

_____

2001: _____

_____

_____

_____

c.   Return on total assets:

2002: _____

_____

_____

2001: _____

_____

_____

_____

Analysis: _____

_____

_____

_____

_____

_____

_____

_____
_____
_____
_____
_____
_____
_____
_____
_____
_____
_____
_____

Analysis: _____
_____
_____
_____
_____
_____
_____
_____
_____
_____
_____
_____

Exercise 20-18
a.   Return on common shareholders' equity:
2002: _____
_____
_____

2001: _____
_____
_____
_____

Name _____

b.   Price earnings ratio, December 31:

2002: _____

_____

_____

_____

2001: _____

_____

_____

_____

c.   Dividend yield:

2002: _____

_____

_____

2001: _____

_____

_____

_____

Name _____

Income Statement Trends For Years Ended December 31, 2005-1999						
2005	2004	2003	2002	2001	2000	1999

Balance Sheet Trends December 31, 2005-1999						
2005	2004	2003	2002	2001	2000	1999

_____

_____

_____

_____

_____

_____

_____

_____

_____

_____

_____

_____

_____

_____

_____

_____

_____

Chapter 20 Problem 20-4A
Part 1 (Continued)

Name _____

Analysis: _____
_____
_____
_____
_____
_____
_____
_____
_____

Part 2

	_____ Company	_____ Company

Profit margin:
_____
_____
_____
_____

Total asset turnover:
_____
_____
_____
_____

Return on total assets:
_____
_____
_____
_____

Return on common shareholders' equity:
_____
_____
_____
_____

Price-earnings ratio:
_____
_____
_____
_____
_____

_____ Company   _____ Company

Dividend yield: _____

_____
_____
_____
_____
_____

Analysis: _____

_____
_____
_____
_____
_____
_____
_____
_____

Transaction	Current Assets	Quick Assets	Current Liabilities	Current Ratio	Acid-Test Ratio	Working Capital

Supporting computations:

Name _____

Fundamental Accounting Principles, 10th Canadian Edition

Name _____

_____
_____
_____
_____
_____
_____
_____
_____

Part 2

Common-Size Comparative Income Statement **For Years Ended December 31, 2002, 2001, and 2000**	*2002*	*2001*	*2000*

	Balance Sheet Data in Trend Percentages For Years Ended December 31, 2002, 2001, and 2000		
	2002	2001	2000

Part 4

Name _____

Income Statement Trends For Years Ended December 31, 2005-1999						
2005	2004	2003	2002	2001	2000	1999

Balance Sheet Trends December 31, 2005-1999						
2005	2004	2003	2002	2001	2000	1999

Name _____

_____
_____
_____
_____
_____
_____
_____
_____
_____
_____
_____
_____
_____
_____
_____
_____
_____
_____

(a) Current ratio: _____
_____
_____
_____

(b) Acid-test ratio: _____
_____
_____
_____

(c) Days' sales uncollected: _____
_____
_____
_____

(d) Merchandise turnover: _____
_____
_____
_____

(e) Days' sales in inventory: _____
_____
_____
_____

(f) Ratio of pledged assets to secured liabilities: _____
_____
_____
_____

(g) Times interest earned: _____
_____
_____
_____

(h) Profit margin: _____
_____
_____
_____

(i) Total asset turnover: _____
_____
_____
_____

Chapter 20   Problem 20-3B
(Continued)

Name _____

(j) Return on total assets:

_____
_____
_____
_____

(k) Return on common shareholders' equity:

_____
_____
_____
_____

Problem 20-4B
Part 1

_____ Company   _____ Company

Current ratio:

_____
_____
_____
_____

Acid-test ratio:

_____
_____
_____
_____

Accounts (and notes) receivable turnover:

_____
_____
_____
_____
_____

Merchandise turnover:

_____
_____
_____
_____

Days' sales in inventory:

_____
_____
_____
_____

Days' sales uncollected:

_____
_____
_____
_____

Analysis: _____
_____
_____
_____
_____
_____
_____
_____
_____
_____

Part 2

_____ Company   _____ Company _____

Profit margin: _____
_____
_____
_____
_____

Total asset turnover: _____
_____
_____
_____
_____

Return on total assets: _____
_____
_____
_____
_____

Return on common shareholders' equity: _____
_____
_____
_____
_____

Price-earnings ratio: _____
_____
_____
_____
_____
_____

_____ Company   _____ Company

Dividend yield: _____

_____

_____

_____

_____

_____

Analysis: _____

_____

_____

_____

_____

_____

_____

_____

_____

Transaction	Current Assets	Quick Assets	Current Liabilities	Current Ratio	Acid-Test Ratio	Working Capital

Supporting computations:

Hope Company
Balance Sheet
December 31, 2002

				Liabilities and	
Assets				**Shareholders' Equity**	
Cash	$		Current liabilities		$
Accounts receivable, net ...			12% bonds payable		
Merchandise inventory			Common shares		
Capital assets, net	_____		Retained earnings		_____
			Total liabilities and		
Total assets	$ _____		shareholders' equity		$ _____

Supporting computations:

	Current Ratio			Acid-Test Ratio		
	Increase	Decrease	No Change	Increase	Decrease	No Change
a. Bought $50,000 of merchandise on account.						
b. Credit sales: $70,000 of merchandise costing $40,000.						
c. Collected a $8,500 account receivable.						
d. Paid a $30,000 account payable.						
e. Wrote off a $2,000 bad debt against the allowance account.						
f. Declared a $1 per share cash dividend on the 20,000 common shares outstanding.						
g. Paid the dividend declared in (f)						
h. Borrowed $25,000 by giving the bank a 60-day, 10% note.						
i. Borrowed $100,000 by placing a 10-year mortgage on the capital assets.						
j. Used $50,000 of proceeds of the mortgage to buy additional machinery.						

Part 2

(i) _____

_____

(ii) _____

_____

(iii) _____

_____

Name _____

(1)

Key figures	NIKE		Reebok	
	%	$	%	$
Cash and equivalents				
Accounts receivable				
Inventory				
Retained earnings				
Cost of sales				
Income taxes				
Revenues (NIKE)				
Net sales (Reebok)				
Total assets				

(2) _____
_____
_____

(3) _____
_____
_____

(4) _____
_____
_____

(5) _____
_____
_____